Prince Saionji

Makers
of the
Modern
World

Prince Saionji
Japan
Jonathan Clements

HH
HAUS HISTORIES

First published in Great Britain in 2008 by
Haus Publishing Ltd
26 Cadogan Court
Draycott Avenue
London SW3 3BX
www.hauspublishing.com

The moral right of the author has been asserted

A CIP catalogue record for this book
is available from the British Library

ISBN 978-1-905791-68-2

Series design by Susan Buchanan
Typeset in Sabon by MacGuru Ltd
Printed in Dubai by Oriental Press
Maps by Martin Lubikowski, ML Design, London

Contents

Note on names   vii
Introduction   I

I   The Life and the Land   II
1   The Black Ships   13
2   Confused Loyalties   23
3   The Meiji Restoration   31
4   *Japonisme*   40
5   The Eastern Liberal News   54
6   Japanism   68
7   The Yellow Peril   81
8   The Taishō Crisis   97

II   The Paris Peace Conference   109
9   The Faults of the Past   III
10   An Anglo-American Peace   127
11   The Shandong Question   137

III   The Legacy   147
12   The Dark Valley   149
13   Last of the *Genrō*   161

Notes   170
Chronology   182
Further Reading   194
Picture Sources   200
Index   202

For Adam Newell
'Young men make wars ...
then old men make the peace.'

Note on names

Names in the book reflect current usage, not the variant spellings utilised in 1919, Hepburn romanisation for Japanese and Pinyin for Chinese – hence Kinmochi instead of Kimmochi, and Shandong instead of Shantung. Name order for Japanese presents the surname first. Reflecting the English-language custom in the 20th century, the text uses the personal name in the style of European monarchy, even though such a policy would appear over-familiar in Japanese. For example, the Taishō Emperor's heir is referred to throughout as Hirohito, although only his reign title as Emperor, Shōwa, would usually be employed in Japan.

Prince Saionji

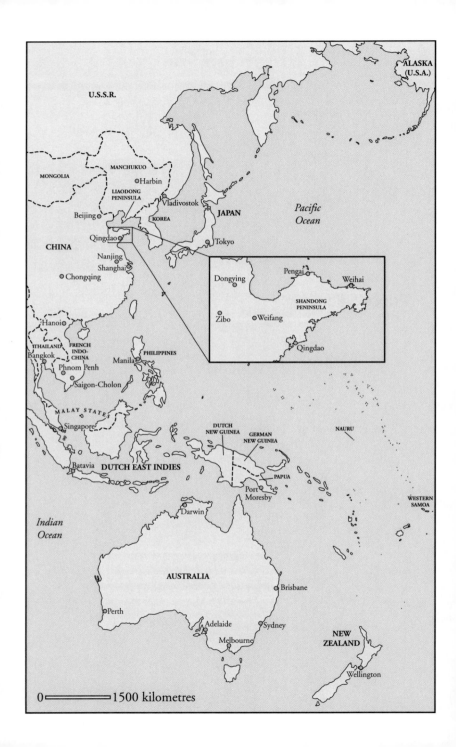

Introduction

In 1896, Stephen Bonsal had been a chargé d'affaires at a Tokyo Legation, and Saionji Kinmochi had been a vice-minister in the Japanese government. Twenty-three years later, Bonsal was an aide to the American delegation at the Paris Peace Conference, and tasked with a diplomatic mission of great delicacy. He was to go to the Paris address of the man who was now Marquis Saionji and verify that the shadowy leader of the Japanese delegation was even in town.

Ushered past two forbidding bodyguards at a house in the Parc Monceau quarter, Bonsal was led to a room suffused with a gentle glow from the daylight outside. He waited for some seconds before he realised that he was not alone. Prince Saionji, who had been standing with unearthly stillness, advanced with an outstretched hand.

The 69-year-old statesman was tall and thin, perhaps too thin – he had only recently recovered from a bout of pneumonia. He wore traditional Japanese clothes in stark contrast to the frock-coated minions who made up the rest of the Japanese delegation. His white hair was cropped close to his head, giving him a military demeanour.

The meeting began with amiable chatter about a mutual

acquaintance from the Tokyo days, before Saionji effortlessly wrong-footed Bonsal by switching into Japanese. Desperately trying to recall the language he had all but forgotten a generation earlier, the high-ranking Bonsal was reduced to a stammering wreck. Although Saionji could have easily continued the conversation in French, which he spoke fluently, he called in an interpreter for the remainder of the meeting.

Bonsal tried to butter Saionji up, mentioning his name in the same breath as some of Japan's greatest reformers and aristocratic leaders. These *genrō*, best translated as 'statesmen', had transformed the Asian nation in mere decades.

Even my most indulgent friends, demurred Saionji, *speak of me only as a half-*genrō.

Trying a different tack, Bonsal recalled a bonsai tree taken from the great Japanese shrine at Ise, to which their colleague Mutsu Munemitsu has once tried to graft shoots from many different countries. Both Bonsal and Saionji saw the tree not just as an experiment in horticulture, but as a political allegory.

He grafted on the sacred stem shafts and cuttings, said Saionji, *of pines from Norway and from Scotland, from Russia and from California. As a result of these shocks there were temporary setbacks, but soon the noble ... pine from Ise prevailed.*

Bonsal returned to report to his boss, Colonel House, that Saionji seemed dishearteningly ready to push Japan's case at the conference.

'You have established the fact,' replied House, 'that the Prince is in Paris, and from "behind the curtain" is pulling the wires that control the dance of his puppets.'[1]

ooooo

Saionji Kinmochi was born on 7 December 1849, in what was then Japan's capital of Kyoto. He was the second son of a minor noble family, the Tokudaiji, adopted at an early age by childless relatives, and raised in an aristocratic world. By the rich standards of its past, imperial Japan had fallen on hard times, but Saionji still enjoyed an upbringing of luxury and privilege. By imperial order, he was a playmate and companion of the prince who would one day become Japan's Meiji Emperor. Born into a Japan that had shunned outside contact for centuries, he reached adulthood during a time of cataclysmic social change in his homeland. He witnessed the humiliation of the old order and the tumult as Japan sought to survive in the modern world. Old enmities and new alliances conspired to create Japan as a modern nation, and Saionji was one of the first generation of Japanese scholars sent to learn from the West.

Happenstance sent him to France, where the young aristocrat became a member of Parisian society, befriending playwrights, authors and future politicians. Wealth kept Saionji in Europe when many of his fellow Japanese students were forced to return, and his prolonged sojourn outside Japan made him an ideal candidate in later life for the role of ambassador and diplomat.

It is necessary to read between the lines in Saionji's life. His three main Japanese biographers were employees or associates who treated him at all times with forelock-tugging deference, and colluded in the maintenance of what historian Lesley Connors has called a 'bland and passive public persona'. It is only in the reminiscences of others that we can see a different approach to the same facts. A cursory glance behind the misty-eyed anecdotes from Saionji's childhood reveals an arrogant and impetuous aristocrat, notorious for an iconoclastic streak since his early teens. Saionji was one of the first Japanese nobles to affect Western dress, to cut his hair and to visit Europe, yet while such innovations are regarded by many writers as signs of his progressive nature, the more cynical reader might see in them a simpler, prosaic youthful rebellion. Saionji once scandalised Tokyo society by proposing that he should marry a woman of the untouchable underclass. It was an important moment in the history of Japanese civil rights, but may also have been little more than a prank – in fact, Saionji never married, instead keeping a series of long-term mistresses. One was with him long enough to be regarded as a common-law wife, others were briefer liaisons glossed over by coy biographers.[2]

Saionji was in his seventies at the time of the Paris Peace Conference, an obscure figure who took a back seat to the main negotiations and gained a reputation as an inscrutable puppet-master. This is how historians usually remember him, as a powerful, cunning statesman of the early 20th century. But even in 1919 there are echoes of his former puckishness. Despite his reputation as a peacemaker and diplomat, it has been somewhat unfairly suggested that Saionji, who arrived at the beginning of March, later than most other diplomats, only agreed to lead the Japanese delegation as an excuse to give his daughter a free trip to Paris. He also arrived in the company of a mistress 50 years his junior, much to the entertainment of the Parisian press.[3]

Saionji has been described as 'the man who Westernised Japan', a strange appellation for someone who spent so long outside his native land. Despite witnessing many famous historical events abroad, luck or design permitted him a series of fortunate absences from critical (and dangerous) moments in Japanese politics. He played a part in the reforging of Japan, but was absent for many of the early domestic *putsches* and feuds that might have ended his career early. He was abroad for much of the era of constitutional scuffles and political assassinations; he fast-tracked into the administration after impressively missing the early cabinet battles, and was conveniently elsewhere when several national scandals broke. As this book details, he officially became Foreign Minister only *after* the embarrassment of the Triple Intervention, left office just *before* the assassination of Queen Min in Korea, and became Prime Minister only *after* the Treaty of Portsmouth.

Sometimes one gets a sense of the young Saionji as a supremely crafty procrastinator, arriving late to meetings just in time to claim the credit. On several occasions, his name was attached to projects for which lower-born associates had done the groundwork – a noble figurehead whose patronage was used to add an invaluable cachet. He is remembered, a trifle misleadingly, as the founder of two universities, as well as a liberal newspaper from which he was forced to resign. In fact, as befitted the dates bracketed by his life, he dwelt in a strange limbo between the old imperial order and modern industrial society. He achieved much, but did so from an inescapable background of privilege, which he was invariably able to twist to his advantage. He was one of the first internationalist Japanese, and became one of the handful of diplomats who formed Japan's first contacts with the outside world.

Throughout his life, Saionji enjoyed a close affinity with France. He was a heartfelt Francophile, whose love for French cologne and Vichy Water remained an indulgence to his dying day. In his youth, the French were the secret backers of his Shōgunal enemies. As a courtier, he chose French as the language most likely to help him get along – at the time, the French had the most powerful army in the world. Graduating from the Sorbonne with a law degree, he became fluent in the language but also witnessed the aftermath of the Franco-Prussian War, which saw a military power laid low by defeat. As a student and then a minor legation official, he lived in France for a decade, becoming the darling of a Parisian literary set enamoured with the new fad for *japonisme*.

Although remembered today as an *éminence grise*, Saionji was once also the dashing young nobleman to whom a Parisian lady admirer dedicated a volume of poetry, whose tall tales of feudal Japan inspired a swashbuckling novel, and who supposedly co-wrote a play performed at the Paris Odéon. In his later diplomatic career, he was unable to stay away from Paris for long, often taking unnecessary detours on flimsy pretexts in order to return to his youthful stomping-grounds. Such visits may have been self-indulgent, but they also gained him great political currency with colleagues such as his former classmate Georges Clemenceau, an association upon which he capitalised at the Paris Peace Conference.

Saionji's political career in Japan was a bewildering whirl of short-lived administrations, from which a concise history such as this can only pluck the merest crumbs of important policy precedents. Saionji was never elected by popular vote – he regarded himself as a caretaker of an infant democratic system that still required patrician stewardship in its early days. His party, the *Seiyūkai*, only agreed under duress to the extension of suffrage to all men over 25 in 1925. Women in Japan did not get the right to vote until 1946, after Saionji's death. Consequently, all his political appointments were made by ministerial or imperial fiat.

Saionji also enjoyed the peculiar position of retaining a cabinet position even when out of office. Through the first decade of the 20th century, he was either a Prime Minister in his own government, or an imperially-appointed Privy Councillor auditing the cabinet of his rival Katsura Tarō – the two men alternated in the Prime Minister's job for over a decade. This semi-permanent position close to the heart of power gave him a unique authority in Japanese politics. On his retirement in 1913, he was asked to become a *genrō*, an imperial adviser whose ability to steer ministerial appointments gave him another role beyond that of the everyday executive. He is remembered in Japan as one of the *genrō* – accorded the status of national heroes – but was actually the last and the youngest of that famous cabal.

When Saionji arrived in Paris in 1919, it was as a statesman who firmly believed in the importance of diplomacy and peace. He was determined to keep Japan out of further war, and resolved to bring it into the international community. In this, he was at odds not only with the unspoken racism of many European delegates, but also with the belligerent sense of entitlement of many within his own government. He was also obliged to speak on behalf of Korea, which at the time was a Japanese colony, much to the annoyance of many Koreans who had vainly hoped that the Peace Conference would restore their sovereignty.

The Japanese arrived at the Paris Peace Conference believing it to be their just reward – after a generation imitating the behaviour of the imperialist powers in the Far East, they hoped to be admitted to their number. Initially, the Conference seemed to welcome them; they had the same number of seats as the Great Powers, and enjoyed strong personal connections, particularly with the French delegates. But some other delegates regarded the Japanese as something of a joke. Many Japanese representatives lacked the necessary English or French to follow the debates in any detail, and Japan's main interest at the Conference – the enshrinement of racial equality in the League of Nations constitution – was rudely shoved aside. As a compromise, Japan received unjust territorial gains at the Conference, to the embarrassment of the leaders and to the great irritation of the Chinese.

The Paris Peace Conference was one of the last tasks of Saionji's long career. In retirement, he continued to fight against the militarist factions who would eventually take over his government. He died believing that Japan was set on a doomed course for war, and was proved right. Much of his contemporary reputation is founded on the post-war years, as Japanese historians searched through the early 20th century for heroes who were not tainted by militarism.

Prince Kinmochi Saionji. Leader of the Japanese delegation to the Paris Peace Conference in 1919

I

The Life and the Land

1
The Black Ships

As one of the oldest and furthest-travelled of the statesmen at Paris, it is not unfair to suggest that Saionji Kinmochi was born in a different world and a radically different environment from that of his fellow politicians, where not even words oblige the reader by meaning what they say. The facts of his early life are obscured behind a mist of court protocols and euphemisms that might lead an inattentive historian to make many basic errors. His birth-date is often erroneously ascribed to October, since he was born in the tenth *lunar* month, at a time before Japan had adopted the Western calendar. His birth year, for complex reasons of tradition, was deliberately misreported as 1847 in order to qualify him for sinecure duties he could not possibly have been old enough to perform. His given name at birth and for much of his childhood was Yoshimaru, and his biological family was not the Saionji but the Tokudaiji. The man he called Father was a step-parent: an ageing, childless relative who died soon after adopting him, for whom Saionji was obliged to perform ancestral sacrifices.

Arguably, at least some of the problems that beset Japan

during Saionji's life were born from similar exasperating insistences on such foggy, intangible facts. Saionji grew up in the imperial capital, Kyoto, but the Emperor of Japan was merely a figurehead. True power rested with the Shōgun in Edo (Tokyo), although legally the Shōgun was merely the Emperor's leading general. Power in Japan was often held obliquely, wielded by nameless officials, 'retired' potentates or elder relatives. When Japan encountered the more direct, concrete laws and institutions of the West, many misunderstandings, indeed many deaths, were to occur as a result of such disengagement between offices and powers.

Saionji himself was to become part of this process. In adult life, he was the kingmaker of Japanese politics, an honoured statesman whose political career often seemed insubstantial, but whose diplomatic achievements were manifold. He died defeated, overwhelmed by the rise of militarism in Japan – his one lasting success could be said to be the endurance and the constitutional position of the Japanese Emperor, for which he toiled unstintingly.

Although remembered as a reformer or even a radical, Saionji was also the inheritor of a long tradition of the Japanese court. Both his real and adopted families were offshoots of the imperial house, whose members had often held important offices. During the reign of the Higashiyama Emperor (r.1675–1710), dwindling finances led the imperial house to plot one of the periodic trimmings of its family tree. An initial plan to force all but one of the sons and daughters of the incumbent Emperor into careers as Buddhist monks and nuns was deemed too severe. As part of a new solution, a Prince Naohito set up the house of Kan'in, of which both the Saionji and Tokudaiji families would become branches.

Like other relatives of the imperial family, the Kan'in

immediately began intrigues to edge their way back into the main line of succession, largely using diplomatic marriages. Consequently, despite 'leaving' the imperial family, the Kan'in menfolk were able to exert new, subtle influence as the uncles and cousins of Naohito's grandson, Emperor Kōkaku (r.1771–1840).

This was nothing unusual in imperial Japan. The men of the Kan'in were merely repeating the diplomacies of their ancestors in the Fujiwara clan, who had gained a veritable monopoly on high court offices in the medieval period. They linked themselves to the emperors by marriage, so that men of their house were grandfathers, fathers-in-law, brothers-in-law and sons-in-law of the emperors. The Confucian rules of propriety, ordering respect for one's elders, ensured that every emperor heard the suits and audiences of his relatives, and imparted great power to the clans.

Tradition also demanded that one should show respect to one's ancestors in the afterlife. Male heirs were required to make offerings to their ancestors – a stipulation so important that no family, even commoners, could afford to let its line of succession peter out. Couples with only female children might ask a son-in-law to take on the family name, effectively adopting him. Couples who were childless, for whatever reason, might instead hope to adopt a relative's boy as their own; it was in this capacity that Saionji obtained his first promotion and palace position, before he was even able to walk.

The infant Saionji was immediately swept up in clan machinations. Since his parents already had an heir ten years his senior, he was of less benefit to his immediate family than he was to their relatives. In 1851 he was officially adopted by childless relatives of the Saionji family, not in an honorific sense, what we might term a godson, but entirely and legally, 'as a real son'. His adoptive father died within the year, his adoptive mother the year after, but by signing him over, at least on paper, his birth parents raised him to the status of son and heir to a noble family. A similar tactic was applied to Saionji's younger brother, who was adopted into a wealthy industrial clan, the Sumitomo.

A major fire in Kyoto in 1854 forced the Saionji family to leave their usual abode and lodge for a while with one of their retainers in the west end of town. This relocation is the origin of one of the doubtful anecdotes about Saionji's life, since it was often claimed that this caused the young boy to become a pupil of the Confucian scholar Nakashima Sōin. In fact, Saionji himself denied this during his own lifetime, instead noting that he was merely impressed, in his new house, by the sight of his next-door neighbour, who would give seminars on the Confucian classics while tending to his garden.[1]

Satsuma was a powerful feudal domain in what is now Kagoshima Prefecture at the south-western tip of Kyūshū. Chōshū was a similarly influential domain that straddled the Shimonoseki Strait between Kyūshū and the main Japanese island of Honshū. The Chōshū rulers had been moved there two centuries earlier in what they regarded as a betrayal by the Tokugawa. Both domains were hotbeds of anti-Shōgunal feeling, and enjoyed unofficial trading connections with the outside world – Satsuma enjoyed suzerainty over the Ryūkyū Islands to the south, allowing unofficial trade with China, while Chōshū was close to Tsushima Island and Korea. Following the Meiji Restoration, these clans came to dominate Japanese government.

Other stories of Saionji's youth are less scholarly. His birth father, deprived of any actual authority by the adoption, but still taking an interest in his son's upbringing, reprimanded him for his reckless ways. Saionji was a playmate and friend of the young crown prince (the future Meiji Emperor), but broke the rules of court propriety by speaking to 'outsiders' – in particular, samurai warriors from the fractious southern domains of Satsuma and Chōshū, who were rightly regarded as suspicious characters by the Kyoto elite. On several occasions he was also caught practising with a sword. Despite Japan's martial past, the Kyoto elite looked down on such brutish displays, particularly in a time of national paranoia.[2]

The tensions in Japan had been caused by several linked problems. The first, and most obvious in the sleepy imperial capital, was the increasing poverty of the warrior class. Two centuries of relative isolation from the outside world had led to an inexorable change in economic conditions. The merchant class, traditionally regarded as the lowliest, had thrived in conditions of peaceful trade. Meanwhile, the samurai warrior elite was sliding into penury with no battles to fight and little reward but stipends for food and lodging, sometimes paid directly in rice. For many, it was a matter of honour – it was unthinkable for a samurai to set aside his warrior-status and work for a living, although such an attitude forced many into vagrancy. Kyoto itself, long a backwater of geisha and monks, acquired a rising crime rate as toughs, beggars and brawlers converged on its sacred precincts. The city attracted an underclass of self-proclaimed samurai, all looking for work, most looking for a fight, ever ready to prove their wounded honour with the swords that were their last possessions. Many of them were *rōnin*, masterless samurai who had lost their lords, either through criminal activity, bereavement or simple cutbacks. All were in search of a change to better their own circumstances, and many found it in slogans based on their idea of loyalty to the Emperor.

The Shōgun, that barbarian-quelling general in distant Edo, ruled Japan in the name of the Emperor, but was failing in his single most important duty. All he had to do to justify his title was keep the foreign barbarians out. Instead, the Shōgun had shown himself to be powerless. The foreign barbarians had already arrived, and they had humiliated Japan.

The culprit was Matthew Calbraith Perry (1794–1858), an ageing Commodore of the American navy, who had been charged by President Millard Fillmore with the task of establishing diplomatic relations with Japan. With a track record as a man of action, having served both in the Mexican War and in the suppression of African slavers, Perry was no diplomat. On the basis of previous attempts by others to open negotiations with Japan, he had concluded that no nation would be able to get a satisfactory answer from Japan unless it turned up with a display of superior military force. Nor was there much point in sticking to Nagasaki, the only port in Japan where limited foreign contact was tolerated. The Americans knew more about this than the Japanese realised, as for the previous four years, the 'Dutch' merchants in Nagasaki had actually been American, trading under a flag of convenience. Instead, overtures should be made direct to the heart of government, which, the Americans had concluded, was not the Emperor in Kyoto, but his Shōgun in Edo.

For Perry, it was merely a matter of time before the British, French or Russians would have the same idea, and he determined to open diplomatic relations as soon as possible. Perry had already visited Okinawa, and built a base on the remote Bonin Islands. On 8 July 1853, he sailed right into the heart of the Shōgun's domain, arriving with two frigates and two sailing vessels at Uraga, perilously close to Edo itself.

In the panicked negotiations that followed, Perry refused to negotiate with underlings, claiming that he was an 'Admiral', and instead sending out his own lieutenants to insist that the Shōgun personally receive a letter from the American

President. Japanese officers begged the Americans to sail to Nagasaki and await a ruling, while the Americans flouted the Shōgun's authority by sending ships to chart Tokyo Bay in full view of the local people. Eventually, he was persuaded to come back for an answer in a year, and the Americans left.

The Japanese government was plunged into chaos. One look at the Black Ships was enough to convince them that the warrior class, whose power was based on their ability to defend Japan, did not stand a chance against the new arrivals. Not even the belligerent samurai in Satsuma thought they should engage the Americans in open battle – instead, the Japanese hatched a scheme to tie up the new arrivals in negotiations for a few years, with the hope that they might be steered into accepting the same kind of limited terms that kept the Chinese and Dutch confined to Nagasaki.

The Chancellor, Takatsukasa Masamichi, even suggested that the situation was not as bad as it first appeared. The Americans had not threatened war; they had merely asked for Japanese ports to be opened for trade and repairs. Mollifying the anxious nobles, Takatsukasa pointed out that Japan already traded, in a very limited extent, with the Chinese and the 'Dutch'. The Americans would simply be one more trading partner – it was not, he argued, the end of the world.[3]

It was less than a month before a second group of unwelcome visitors arrived in Japan. Four ships under Vice-Admiral Evfimy Vasilyevich Putiatin (1803–84) arrived in Nagasaki, bearing a letter from the Russian Minister for Foreign Affairs. The Russians tried a softer approach, noting in a polite letter that, unlike the Americans, they had decided to drop anchor in Nagasaki as a mark of respect for Japanese law. However, they wanted the same things – trade concessions and diplomatic relations – and they had the same engines of persuasion

– steam-powered warships, which they took great pleasure in demonstrating.

The Japanese were utterly at a loss. Although firearms had been known in Japan since the 16th century, the country had effectively given up the gun at the end of its last civil war. With peace restored and a Shōgun in charge of defending the land from external aggressors, there had simply been no perceived need for modern weaponry. Japanese military readiness had remained at an almost medieval level ever since, and the country was thoroughly unprepared for the new threat. The best that Japanese tacticians could offer was that suicide squads be set up ready to swarm over enemy warships, or that coastal domains should plant more bamboo groves, in the hope that thick forests would somehow protect the villages beyond from artillery.

Some simply turned to bluster. In Kyoto, the aristocracy continued to brag of their prowess with traditional weaponry. The young Saionji reputedly questioned an archery expert, who had boasted that bows and arrows were superior to rifles. The argument was based on the comparison of the rate of fire between a skilled archer and a musketeer struggling to reload, and on the poor accuracy of musketry. In his first recorded modernist statement, however, Saionji noted that archery took seven or eight years to master, whereas entire armies of soldiers might be trained to shoot their guns in mere months.[4]

Both Perry and Putiatin would be back. In March 1854, the returning Perry was presented with the Convention of Kanagawa, which granted most of the demands made by the American president, and opened the ports of Shimoda and Hakodate to American trade. The Russians were back later in the year, and, tiring of waiting for a respectful reply to their overtures from Nagasaki, sailed instead with a state-of-the-art warship to Osaka Bay, perilously close to the imperial capital. They were edged back to Shimoda, a port on Japan's east coast that was ravaged soon after by an earthquake measuring 8.4 on the Richter scale, followed by an ominous tsunami. Perhaps as a result of the Russian and Japanese co-operation in the aftermath, perhaps in recognition of the Russians' behaviour, or simply because Russia and Japan had mutual border issues to discuss in the northern island of Sakhalin, the Russians got a much better deal. They received trading privileges in three ports, with Nagasaki added to the pair that the Americans had already secured.

Further treaties swiftly followed. Concerned about a clause offering Russian 'help' to the Japanese in case of American aggression, the British sought clarification, and ended up with a Treaty of Anglo-Japanese Friendship, partly as a result of a translation error. The greatest gains were made over the two ensuing years by Townsend Harris, the American consul sent to Shimoda as part of the deal secured by Perry. By 1858, Harris had successfully negotiated the Treaty of Amity and Commerce, which fixed import-export duties, opened five more ports to the Americans, including Edo itself, and established diplomatic relations. In a crushing blow to the Shōgun's authority, Harris's treaty also permitted American citizens to live in the newly opened ports and granted them extraterritoriality – the right to be tried by their own courts, effectively freeing them from the jurisdiction of local laws.

The effect of these humiliations took a while to reach Kyoto. It was first felt at the treaty ports themselves, where local lords complained about the Shōgun's incompetence. The first real sign of it came when the Shōgun, hoping to maintain the appearance of following orders, attempted to justify his decisions by seeking the Emperor's approval – a nod from the Emperor, of course, would imply that the Shōgun was continuing to do his duty. While that established a precedent of its own, the more immediately apparent result of the Unequal Treaties, as they came to be known, was that Kyoto's growing population of itinerant samurai finally had something to fight about. Those with allegiance to the Shōgunate were increasingly defensive about their position. Those with allegiance to powerful domains saw it as an excuse for the Shōgun to be fired – perhaps to be replaced with one of their own men.

2
Confused Loyalties

Court life continued for the young Saionji, who had climbed a promotional 'ladder' of vaguely-defined sinecures. In 1853, although barely old enough to walk, he was appointed Chamberlain, and in 1857 became a Minor General of the Right Imperial Guard – his duties largely being little more than being an approved playmate of Mutsuhito, the young prince who was nominated as heir to the throne in 1860. Court protocol demanded that a member of Saionji's adopted family be installed as a player of the *biwa*, a harp-like musical instrument at which he was expected to excel, but which he never liked. He continued to read books that were proscribed by the court, including a Chinese translation of Thomas Milner's *English History*, which somehow reached him through unknown channels.

Rising to Middle General of the Right Imperial Guard, Saionji was ordered to attend the palace daily, but was excused from 'miscellaneous duties' – many of his fellow young nobles were little more than waiters for the young prince, but Saionji appears to have enjoyed the favour of the prince in tense times.

One night in 1860, carpenters repairing one of the Kyoto palaces accidentally started a fire, which spread to a nearby bamboo hedge, causing the stalks to heat up, dry out and finally crack in a succession of loud bangs. The noise was immediately mistaken for gunfire by the courtiers, in an incident when, once more, Saionji was at the prince's side, refusing to desert his post, even though it was later revealed to be a false alarm.[1]

More genuine violence, however, had been brought to bear in the ongoing factional struggle over how to deal with foreign aggressors. Tokugawa Nariaki, lord of the powerful Mito domain, tried to draw the Emperor and Shōgun into dialogue – essentially to admit that the foreign problem was impossible to counter with old-fashioned methods, and would instead require a programme of national reforms. But Tokugawa Nariaki's own Mito countrymen saw things differently, joining forces with fellow samurai from Satsuma in 1860 to assassinate Ii Naosuke, a prominent voice in support of gradual change. In a final attempt to keep Emperor and Shōgun united, the Chamberlain Iwakura Tomomi tried to broker a marriage between the Shōgun and the Emperor's younger sister, but the plan failed.

The foreign problem escalated in an unlikely fashion in the late summer of 1862, when a group of British merchants refused to dismount from their horses at the approach of a samurai lord's retinue. Charles Lennox Richardson, a trader from Shanghai, was killed in the scuffle that ensued, and depicted back in Britain as the innocent victim of brutish natives. In fact, Richardson had already enjoyed a certain notoriety in Shanghai for bullying behaviour towards locals, and was likely to have been the instigator of his own demise. Whatever the true facts of the incident, the British government demanded reparations from both the Shōgun and from Satsuma, the domain whose samurai had lashed out. Satsuma refused, leading to a brief but momentous incident the following year. With reparations still not forthcoming, Royal Navy warships opened fire on the south Japanese port of Kagoshima. The two-day exchange of bluff insults, followed by cannon-fire, was just one of many petty skirmishes fought by the British in the 19th century, and resulted in the destruction of several Satsuma vessels and some 500 houses in Kagoshima, which had already been evacuated in the expectation of hostilities. Conversely, the same incident is still remembered in Japan as the Anglo-Satsuma 'War', and regarded as a victory for the Japanese, whose constant artillery barrage kept the British from coming ashore, and who never did hand over or execute the assassins. In reality, commerce won out, with Satsuma paying the indemnity demanded, but also agreeing a lucrative deal to buy new warships from the British.

Far from keeping the foreigners out, the Shōgun was obliged to look on as Satsuma signed trading deals with the hated new arrivals. Back in Kyoto in an atmosphere of excitement, Saionji and his fellow courtiers were ordered to wear swords – Saionji's once-forbidden hobby was now compulsory, by imperial command.[2]

The Emperor Kōmei lost his patience with the Shōgun in 1863, marking the New Year by sending envoys to Edo with a strongly-worded letter, calling for a plan to remove all foreigners from Japanese soil. As an indication of how seriously the Emperor was taking it, his envoy insisted on long-forgotten protocols that placed the Shōgun in an inferior position during the hearing. Mere weeks later, the Shōgun visited the Emperor in person – the first time a Shōgun had been to

Kyoto in 200 years. If he was hoping to persuade the Emperor to tone down his rhetoric, he was out of luck – on 11 March 1863 the Emperor issued an 'Order to Expel Barbarians', setting an impossible two-month deadline.

While most Shōgunal officials fretted over a means of talking the Emperor out of it, or at least saving face with some additional proclamations that lessened the impact, the feudal domain of Chōshū took the Emperor at his word. In June 1863, Chōshū warships, ironically supplied by America, began a series of attacks on foreign shipping in the Shimonoseki

> The subjugation of the hated foreigner is the greatest of the national tasks facing us.
>
> THE KŌMEI EMPEROR

Strait, the vital channel that linked Japan's Inland Sea to the sea-route to China. Chōshū set upon American, French and Dutch shipping, and was soon subject to retaliatory bombardments in July and August from several foreign naval expeditions.

'Loyalism' in the Imperial capital existed in many strange forms. Chōshū representatives petitioned the throne for a pardon for some of their number in 1864, only to be refused. Instead of accepting the will of the Emperor, they regarded his true intent as having been twisted by corrupt ministers. A group assembled in a Kyoto restaurant where they plotted direct (i.e. violent) action, only to be ambushed and killed by the Shinsengumi, a group of fanatical Shōgunate supporters. When news of the tavern murders reached Chōshū, the domain responded with a 1,000-strong army. Its numbers soon swollen by the ever-present *rōnin*, the force was soon camped outside Kyoto and demanding that the Emperor see sense. Had they been successful, Chōshū's plans would have amounted to a *coup d'état* – its soldiers plotted to set fire to the city, using the confusion to assassinate ministerial enemies, wreak revenge on the Shinsengumi, and to drag the Emperor away to Chōshū, there to issue a series of edicts placing Chōshū men in charge of the country.

The various gangs of 'loyalists' infesting Kyoto were impossible to control. A Chōshū force, numbering several hundred, launched a full-scale assault on the Hamaguri Gate early in the morning of 20 August 1864. The palace residents were awoken by the sound of artillery and gunfire, and prepared for evacuation in a panic. The teenage Saionji and other courtiers were geared up as best as possible to resist – tying back their sleeves and donning straw sandals. Swords in hand, they would have been little use against the musket-wielding samurai outside. Several courtiers began a plan to escape in boarded palanquins, although that plan was quelled by a minister who realised that the fleeing nobles would probably be killed in the crossfire. Instead, the imperial courtiers cowered inside their palace as fires raged along the avenues outside. Emperor Kōmei waited calmly for the situation to resolve itself, but his 12-year-old son Mutsuhito, the future Emperor Meiji, was understandably terrified.[3]

August is a scorchingly hot month in Kyoto. It is perhaps no surprise that the battles favoured the early riser and the night owl. On the night of the 21st, the commander of the palace defences was shocked to find 300 men in the inner courtyard, hoping to steal the imperial palanquin. He ordered an immediate evacuation, and in the ensuing panic, a drowsy Prince Mutsuhito was dragged from his bed by ladies-in-waiting. Fears ran so high that the simple breaking of a jar nearby was mistaken for gunfire.

Such confused loyalties also extended to the Japanese state's first attempts at foreign diplomacy. While Kyoto descended into chaos, a Shōgunal mission to France ran into unexpected problems. Instead of gaining the desired agreements, its leader faced a series of French complaints over the Shimonoseki Strait incident. He unwisely accepted French demands, signed an agreement, and then returned to Japan, perhaps in the realisation that he was in enough trouble already, and need not seek similar difficulties in Britain. Of course, back in Japan, the Shōgun refused to ratify the ambassador's promises – a reaction regarded by the foreign powers as yet another devious Japanese obfuscation.

With the Strait still closed and Chōshū still defiant, the French, British and Dutch (with a token American presence) mounted a combined show of strength, bombarding the coastline before landing troops. Chōshū surrendered and was ordered to pay $3 million in damages – of course, the buck was immediately passed to the Shōgun, whose inability to afford it led to further concessions and trade deals.

By this point, the Kōmei Emperor was making demonstrations of his own. He ordered troops to drill before an audience at the palace, and made several conspicuous pilgrimages to the shrines of ancient war heroes. He even let it be known that he was considering taking personal charge of the project to expel barbarians, which only served to agitate the rival factions even more. Some ministers began talks with Chōshū representatives over how they might 'help' the Emperor in this new endeavour. He issued a new proclamation, calling for national unity against the new aggressors: 'The subjugation of the hated foreigner is the greatest of the national tasks facing us. It will finally become possible only if we raise forces with which to chastise them. However, it is not my wish that the expulsion of foreigners be carried out recklessly. I ask you, rather, to evolve a suitable plan with due deliberation and report it to me.'[4]

An exasperated Shōgun sent a military expedition to remind the Chōshū samurai who was boss. This appeared to have the opposite effect, first among the other domains, which were slow to provide manpower against a lord whose strong stance they admired. It also led to a regime change in Chōshū that put a new faction in charge. These new men were not merely opposed to the Shōgun, but had secretly visited Britain and were ready to introduce modern military training to a domain that could now legitimately see itself as threatened by both foreigners and its own government.

No matter the precise colour of one's 'loyalty', the anti-foreign camp in Japan was soon proved right. Far from containing the foreign problem, the latest concessions only invited more. On 16 November 1865, the British, French, Americans and Dutch were back again, with nine warships. This time they were off the port of Hyōgo, near Osaka, demanding imperial assent to the previous treaties, and the opening of the port. In compensation, they were prepared to write off $2 million of the Shimonoseki indemnity, but if the Shōgunate refused, they were prepared to take their case to the Emperor himself, 'amid gunsmoke and a rain of bullets'.[5] During the ten-day grace period allotted to the Japanese, the Shōgun urged the Emperor to accept the conditions. As an admission of his failure to do his own duty, he also tendered his resignation, although it was not accepted.

By 1866, the rival southern domains of Satsuma and Chōshū had settled their differences and joined forces. Meanwhile, in Edo, the Shōgunate was seeking military advice (and the concomitant trade) from the French, which only helped accentuate the battle lines between the British-supported southern domains and French-supported Edo. A second Shōgunal assault on south Japan was beaten back by superior forces and technology – the man charged with defending Japan from foreigners could now no longer beat other Japanese. Mercifully, perhaps, the old Shōgun died in the summer of 1866. In circumstances that remain suspicious, the Emperor did not long outlive him, succumbing to a sudden and unexpected bout of smallpox later in the same year.

His heir was Mutsuhito, a 16-year-old boy already at the centre of the new power struggle. Among the domains, Satsuma and Chōshū hoped to supplant the new Shōgun, while a third domain, Tosa, instead hoped to defuse the crisis by re-asserting the authority of the Emperor himself.

ooooo

During the period when factional struggles drew Japan ever closer to civil war, Saionji became the centre of a new clique at the palace, focused not on war, but on learning. Every few weeks, he would host a meeting at his mansion, where several renowned poets would read and comment on works in the old style. Soon after the opening of the port of Hyogo to foreigners, however, the poetry sessions began to move onto discussions of current affairs, and invited 'teacher-guests' would hold forth on political subjects. Although the group was soon disbanded as its host was drawn into other events, it would form the seeds of one of Saionji's best known legacies – the Ritsumeikan University.

3
The Meiji Restoration

The civil war, usually referred to as the Meiji Restoration, was a triumph of Japanese court etiquette in which meanings are so difficult to pin down. *Every* side claimed to be loyalists. The Shōgun and his Tokugawa vassals were loyal to their posts, as servants of the Emperor. The samurai of Satsuma and Chōshū were loyal to the Emperor, insofar as they regarded it as their duty to supplant the incompetent Tokugawa. Meanwhile, the likes of the Tosa samurai either tried to patch up relations with the Shōgun, or argued that the Shōgunate should be abolished and the Emperor 'returned' to his position as head of state – a problematic argument since few emperors in recorded history had ever been anything more than figureheads. A final group presented an even worse threat to the old order – drunk on Western idealism, the peasants and lower classes were agitating for full democracy, a parliamentary system with rule by the people that risked overturning all of the other classes.

Other problems arose from unsuspected directions, only serving to bolster the arguments of those who thought no good could come of foreign contact. The continued pressure from outside had led to an unexpected outbreak of trouble *inside* Japanese borders. As a side-effect of the extraterritoriality agreement with foreigners, a church had been built in Nagasaki. Much to everyone's surprise, it soon attracted Japanese worshippers, who revealed that they were 'Hidden Christians', the descendants of converts who had kept their beliefs secret for over two centuries. Christianity was still illegal in Japan, and the Hidden Christians were soon agitating for foreign support for their own freedom of worship. Despite pressure from his French military advisors, the Shōgun firmly restated Christianity's illegal status, which in turn led to protests to the Emperor from the British minister Sir Harry Parkes.

Back in Kyoto, the Emperor gained a new adviser, Iwakura Tomomi (1825–83), a statesman who had previously been discredited, but whose strong views on reform had finally found a willing audience with the change in ruler – so willing, in fact, that Iwakura's enemies whispered, without evidence, that he had arranged for Emperor Kōmei to be poisoned. Like Saionji, Iwakura was the adopted son of a minor courtier. He was also a protégé of Takatsukasa Masamichi, the chancellor who had cautioned against over-reaction to the foreign threats. He opposed the Unequal Treaties and supported continued unity of purpose between the Emperor and Shōgun, leading radicals to accuse him of being a Shōgunal sympathiser.

While Satsuma and Chōshū continued to plot the overthrow and replacement of the Shōgun, other domains sent representatives to Kyoto to arrange a different regime change – to head off the southern rebels by reasserting the power of the Emperor himself. Eventually, Satsuma and Chōshū were co-opted into this new group, with a secret communiqué from the court ordering them to overthrow the Shōgun. But even as they prepared to do so, the Shōgun pre-empted them by offering his resignation.

It is unclear who was acting on what demands. The Shōgun's offer of his resignation and the Emperor's demand for it seem to have crossed in the post. In the south, foreign ambassadors were informed that the Emperor, and not the Shōgun was now the head of state. The Shōgunal system, which had ruled Japan in the Emperor's name for half a millennium, had come to a sudden stop. This was the Meiji Restoration, re-asserting Imperial authority.[1]

It did not, however, make Japan's problems go away. 'Loyalists' who backed the Shōgun refused to accept the decision, instead blaming Satsuma intrigues, which they determined to resist by force of arms. Meanwhile, the ex-Shōgun Yoshinobu still clung to his old authority, informing a baffled audience of Western ambassadors that he was still in charge of foreign relations while the new government found its feet. It soon became plain that Yoshinobu's 'resignation' had not been intended as an abrogation of powers, but as a political gesture that signified his willingness to be included in a reformed power structure, rather than be removed from it.[2]

The seizure of Kyoto by forces loyal to Satsuma and Chōshū had turned the old order on its head. The former 'rebels' were now calling themselves defenders of the Emperor; the Shōgun was now the leader of a 'rebel' army, marching on the imperial city. Even among the retainers of the sides, there was confusion as to where loyalties precisely lay. An old samurai from the Shōgunate camp requested a meeting with imperial representatives, and somehow found himself begging an audience, including the young Saionji, to see the Shōgun's point of view. Barely out of his teens, Saionji demanded that the man remonstrate with his own lord. *If the Shōgun is resolved to appeal to arms*, Saionji is supposed to have said, *why do not you, who are loyal to the Throne, remonstrate with him at the risk of your life, or even … death?*[3]

It was Saionji who observed, either through genuine belief or political pragmatism, that the behaviour of the rebels was born out of loyalty to the Emperor, and was not a mere 'vendetta', as their critics would have it. 'You have seen the point young man. You have seen it well, Saionji!' said an approving Iwakura.[4]

The imperial capital had been threatened on many occasions in the past, and protocols were already in place to move the Emperor to a place of seclusion in times of strife. But the landmark nature of the coming battle with the Shōgun was realised by all, and it was decided not to simply move the Emperor to a nearby mountain retreat as in the past, but to cut a corridor south. Should the imperial army meet with defeat against the Shōgun, the Emperor was 'free' to flee further to the south, to Chōshū territory, where he still might be used as a bargaining-counter.

Clearing the way southwards would require the occupation of the nearby city of Tanba – an enterprise that fell to a force under the command of the 19-year-old Saionji.[5] He was the nominal leader of a band of Chōshū and Satsuma samurai, perhaps a compromise candidate put in place to remind the rival groups of their supposed loyalty to a higher office. Although his youthful practice of horsemanship stood him in good stead in his new command, he was less successful at straightforward logistics. There had been no time to bestow Saionji with a Commander-General's sword of office, ceremonial banner, or, it seems, any proper provisions. Instead, couriers ran ahead of the main army, hoping to secure provisions and equipment from the villages on the route; Saionji's first military command arrived in their first billet with very little food.[6]

Saionji's mission was uncertain – much of the action in his campaign seemed to centre on determining which of the fiefs in his path were true supporters of the Emperor, and which were preparing to ambush him. Retreating supporters of the Shōgun spread rumours to impede the advance of the Emperor's troops, and local lords remained unpredictable. One came out in immediate support of Saionji, while a second fled. The escaped lord's castle, Kameoka, was an important stronghold for securing the Emperor's possible escape route, leading Saionji to draw up his troops ready to attack it. But the troops inside the castle had no will to resist with their own lord already on the run, and Kameoka Castle soon surrendered.

> As I was ... only a youth of 19, I could not have had a philosopher's insight into the general trend of the times. I certainly cannot talk as if I had but I felt at least that the overthrow of the Shōgunate must and could be achieved.
>
> SAIONJI KINMOCHI[7]

The nearby Sasayama castle put up a stronger resistance, leading Saionji to call for local volunteers for the coming battle. In this encounter, it would seem that preparation was nine-tenths of victory. Several hundred samurai from each side met on the road to Sasayama, only for the defenders to immediately surrender. They had, it was said, never intended to fight – although their weapons were confiscated, they were immediately freed, and their leader even volunteered to accompany Saionji on his advance.[8]

With the Emperor enjoying physical support from Satsuma and Chōshū, the Shōgun's own backers seemed to have little energy for the fight. The Shōgun's powerlessness had already been ably demonstrated – it seems that the mere presence of troops loyal to the Emperor was often enough to cause locals to re-evaluate their own 'loyalty'.

The lord of Sasayama was left unmolested after agreeing to sign an oath in blood (an everyday occurrence for the Japanese nobility) in which he swore fealty to the Emperor. Soon afterwards, Saionji reached Fukuchiyama, which similarly surrendered without incident. By this time, he had gained an impressive imperial banner, bearing the images of the sun and the moon on a red field, and held aloft by a group of celebrity sumō wrestlers.

After the threats and scuffles of previous years, Saionji's own experience of the civil war seems remarkably gentlemanly. It is easy to see cowardice and hypocrisy in the behaviour of the men who caved in before his advance, but that would often be unfair. Some, it is true, had no interest in fighting. Others knew that the fight was already over, that the Emperor was now in charge. The cynics might phrase things differently, that the cunning Satsuma and Chōshū had finally carried out the plan they had been nursing for so many years, to defeat their enemies by the simple expedient of capturing the Emperor.

The murders and looting of recent times had been done in the name of misguided loyalties, but did not reflect the attitudes of all samurai. The rebels had been largely fighting the absence of true authority; when one was presented to them, they fell back into line.[9]

In that regard, Saionji may have been helped by the cunning of Iwakura Tomomi who had realised the power of symbolism. Saionji's banner was one of many commissioned by Iwakura, using cloth bought in the silk markets of Kyoto. A banner similar to Saionji's was raised by the imperial troops fighting the Shōgun at Toba to the east. Although some fire was exchanged, and there were a few casualties, the battle soon fizzled out in a similar manner. The imperial banner was incontrovertible proof that Shōgun's troops were fighting in opposition to the Emperor they claimed to serve. Not even the Shōgun himself could bring himself to actually charge against the Emperor's flag. Shōgunate forces fled the field, and the Shōgun briefly hid aboard an American warship, before fleeing north on one of his own vessels.[10]

The victory at Toba secured all of southern and western Japan for the Emperor's forces. Effectively, it rendered Saionji's campaign irrelevant, since it was now unlikely that the Emperor would require an escape route after all. Regardless, Saionji pressed on, his army largely enjoying their substantial list of victories won without a shot fired. History repeated itself at several more strongholds, with local samurai loading their weapons and giving every intention of preparing to resist, only to offer their surrender as soon as Saionji appeared ready to commit to battle. Notably, many of them came out to greet Saionji wearing old-fashioned clothes and wearing only swords; the elite often still exhibited a great distaste for the modern developments that had led to the conflict in the first place.

After two weeks of marching, Saionji reached his final objective in Kizuki. His soldiers were sent home, and he returned by ship to Osaka, where the Meiji Emperor was inspecting the navy. Perhaps with genuine praise, perhaps because he was already a familiar face to the courtiers and other military leaders were still pressing north, Saionji was welcomed as a conquering hero. Although brawlers in search of a fight may have been disappointed, he was credited with achieving great military objectives with only minor casualties. For Saionji himself, however, the campaign was not completely successful. His staff officer was chastised for 'avarice' – presumably some form of otherwise unmentioned looting. Furthermore, one of his logistics officers committed suicide after failing to arrange enough labourers for an unspecified task.

The campaign against the Shōgun continued elsewhere. Edo itself fell without a fight, but samurai in the northern domain of Echigo were less willing to give up. Prepared, as ever, for actual combat, the imperial government put Saionji in charge of a new army, only to disband it due to a change in strategies. Instead, he was placed in charge of a new division of several hundred Satsuma men, and sent north. This time, he dawdled, receiving a proper commission from the Emperor in person, and waiting out floods and bad weather where appropriate, eventually reaching Echigo in a British steamer chartered to speed up his arrival.

Saionji and his men expected less of an easy time in Echigo. Saionji first appeared at the front disguised as a sergeant, although his later behaviour displayed a greater degree of recklessness. He developed a reputation with his men for fearlessly riding out to the front to check on them. Perhaps this was born from his relatively danger-free experiences in the south, or from simple foolhardiness: it is difficult to say. Soon, he was urged by his own subordinates to take greater care for his own safety.

Nagaoka Castle fell to the Imperial forces, but not without a bitter fight. Realising that the Echigo area could see several similar battles, the government sent further reinforcements, led by an Imperial prince. Unable to enjoy a commanding position over a prince of the blood, Saionji was edged down the hierarchy into a position more befitting his status – that of chief of the general staff.

Although he cannot have known it at the time, it was the end of Saionji's military career, such as it had been. While the battles continued to rage over the mastery of Echigo, Saionji was kept away from the front line. Finally, in the autumn of 1868, Echigo was pacified. The fighting pushed ever northwards, but Saionji was left behind, ordered to assume a new role as the governor of Echigo province.

For the young Saionji, it spelled disaster. Swept up in events throughout the Meiji Restoration, he had gone from obscure courtier, to member of the inner circle, to victorious general. Now, suddenly, his reward was a dull administrative post in a remote province, away from the action and liable to keep him busy for years.

Saionji had always planned to move away from court life, but had hoped to study abroad. In the days before the outbreak of war, he had already discussed with an approving Iwakura the need for bright young Japanese men to learn from America and Europe, in order to strengthen their homeland. Saionji had rather hoped to be one of them.[11]

Although fighting on the Japanese mainland was over, elements of the Shōgun's navy led by Admiral Enomoto Takeaki fled north to the island of Hokkaidō. There, they set up the short-lived Republic of Ezo, an island stronghold proclaiming its independence from Imperial rule. Hedging their bets, several of their French military advisers 'resigned' their commissions in order to follow Enomoto. However, Ezo's fleet was defeated over several months in the prolonged Battle of Hakodate, ending in May 1869 with an Imperial victory.

Accordingly, with the fighting still raging in the far north, Saionji boldly left his new responsibilities and travelled to Edo, now renamed Tokyo, to resign his commission. He successfully argued that he was of better use abroad, and was awarded a small pension in recognition of his military achievements. He then began preparations for learning a foreign language and leaving Japan behind, to serve his country in the lands beyond.

4

Japonisme

Back in Kyoto, Saionji briefly flirted with founding a school, convening his pre-revolutionary study group under the title of Ritsumeikan – the Hall Establishing Destiny.[1] However, it soon drew up to a hundred visitors per seminar, and seems to have been regarded as a potential breeding-ground for dangerous ideas. The school was shut down in 1869 by order of the Kyoto Prefecture government, and Saionji was grounded in his home for a week in punishment for returning to Kyoto without prior permission.[2]

Choices of foreign study in Meiji Japan were as confused as loyalties to the Emperor. Many studied classical Chinese, but only as a dead language – the modern Japanese believed they had little to learn from the nation that had been humiliated in the Opium Wars with the European powers. For the centuries of isolation, the only official visitors to Japan had been Dutch traders in Nagasaki, and *Rangaku*, 'Dutch Studies', remained the Japanese term for all foreign knowledge.

Saionji, however, chose to learn French, the language spoken by the military advisers of his enemy, the Shōgun. He was encouraged in this by Ōmura Masujirō, a Chōshū general who had previous experience of fighting Shōgunate troops. It seems that Saionji, like many other Japanese, continued to regard the French as the nation most worthy of emulation, despite their being on the losing side of the war – a sure sign of how close-run the victors thought the conflict had been. Diplomatically, the French had disassociated themselves from the 'rogue officers' who had lent their support to the Republic of Ezo, and strategically, they were then regarded as the most powerful military nation in Europe, and hence the world.

Primarily with an interest in military development, and in the establishment of a truly modern Japanese army, Saionji began his French studies in Tokyo. To do so, he applied for permission from the Emperor to give up his name and court titles, enrolling in a college under a pseudonym he had lifted from his favourite play.

Saionji's biographers look upon his romantic indiscretions with an indulgent eye. Supposedly by accident, he donated a fish to fellow diners at his college without realising that it was accompanied by a message to him from a geisha girl. Now 20 years old and unmarried, Saionji controversially suggested that he should marry a woman from the underclass, instead of a court lady. It is unclear whether he had a particular lady in mind, or if he was making a brash point about Japan's allegedly classless society in the aftermath of the Restoration. Much to the scandal of the court, he was also the first to don Western garb, cutting off his topknot, styling his hair 'like a Dutchman', and arriving at court wearing Western-style trousers and a frock coat.[3]

Although nothing came of Saionji's marriage offer, it seems to have been in keeping with the mood of the times. The old feudal system was on the verge of disappearing, with the clans themselves overseeing their own abolition. Satsuma,

Chōshū, Tosa and Hizen, all clans that had fought in the civil war, now memorialised the Meiji Emperor with a suggestion that the old clan system should be replaced by modern prefectures – this was put into effect in 1871.

Saionji, however, was leaving the centre of the new order for Nagasaki, the notorious south-western port that had been the only point of contact with the world outside Japan until the coming of the Unequal Treaties. There, he joined a group of students intent on learning foreign languages ready for study abroad. To many of his fellow courtiers now struggling for posts in Kyoto and Tokyo, it must have seemed like an act of career suicide. However, Saionji's decision was to prove to have a lasting impact on his future promotions. As his friend and biographer Takekoshi Yosaburō put it: 'All those who got into important offices of the Government, and were satisfied with themselves have, excepting four or five able men, ended their more or less useful lives as the grass withers and the trees die. The Prince [Saionji] alone continues to live an active life ... because with firm resolution he discarded immediate interests and went abroad.'[4]

Saionji's journey to France took him eastward, leaving Yokohama on the ss *Costa Rica*, in the company of over 30 other students. The journey was not undertaken in good weather, and the inexperienced travellers had to contend with storms and high seas. Saionji and the others were encouraged to busy themselves writing letters home, and assured that they would be able to post them within a few days, when the *Costa Rica* was scheduled to rendezvous with a mail steamer heading in the opposite direction. Saionji did not take the suggestion seriously, and the shock he felt when the ship turned up, right on time, in precisely the predicted place, is palpable in his letters home from San Francisco.

Modern navigation and timekeeping were not the only surprises in store for Saionji. He was dazzled by the bustle of San Francisco, its tall buildings and its paved boulevards. *I must remember*, he wrote home stoically, *to maintain my objectivity.*[5]

Many of his fellow students dispersed at San Francisco for destinations in the Americas, but Saionji's route took him to the east coast, via Washington DC. The Japanese nobles in the party were presented to President Ulysses S Grant, at a meeting that charmed Saionji with its lack of similarity to stultifying Japanese imperial protocol. *It is totally different*, he wrote, *from what happens when a foreigner is presented at the court. The plainness is very pleasing.* His letters home reported less on meeting the American president, and more on his awe-struck impressions of American women, whose low-cut dresses and shameless presence at social gatherings struck the Japanese student as agreeably scandalous.

A second ship took him across the Atlantic to England, in the company of an affable group of fellow passengers. Saionji's letters, despite his desire to remain aloof, betray a rising fascination and respect for Western technology and civilisation, although there were still occasions when he found the Europeans to be baffling. As his ship neared the docks, a child he had befriended on board tried to kiss him goodbye. Saionji evaded the kiss, laughed in the Japanese manner that denotes embarrassment rather than amusement, and scared the child so much that she burst into tears. The incident served to remind Saionji that he was still among barbarians with, as he put it, *barbarian customs.*[6]

Saionji was in London for 13 days, on a tourist trail that took in the best that the British capital had to offer – museums, London Zoo, and the many great parks. His itinerary included the fabled Crystal Palace, still a monument to Victorian engineering, and a location he cryptically described as the Hall of Heroes – possibly Westminster Abbey. Saionji was astounded by the sight of the Victorian gentry taking the air in wide-open green spaces in the centre of the city: *They stroll grandly and as they please in a sure sign of civilisation*, he wrote. *It makes me feel no better than an animal.*[7]

With the authority of the Meiji Emperor barely understood outside Japan, some of the most influential Japanese in Europe were retainers of the old Satsuma fief. Saionji was able to see first-hand how the Satsuma domain's representatives had been behaving during Japan's troubles. Despite the prohibition on travelling abroad, the fief of Satsuma had been sending representatives in secret to France, where their ambassadors enjoyed diplomatic status under the misleading claim that they hailed from the 'Kingdom of the Ryūkyū Islands'. Although Japan was now supposedly unified under the Emperor, Saionji found that the Japanese booth at a London trade fair sat next to one purportedly belonging to Ryūkyū, and manned by Satsuma retainers.[8]

Saionji finally reached Paris on 27 May 1871, to find a very different series of surprises from the peaceful idyll of London. Instead of the capital of the world's greatest power, Saionji arrived in a city of barricades and curfews, with danger on the streets and a power-struggle within the government itself.

In 1870 Napoleon III had rushed into battle against a coalition of German states, initiating the Franco-Prussian War. The Germans, supplied by efficient railroads and using modern Krupp artillery, soon outmatched the French, and made swift advances into eastern France, culminating in the Battle of Sedan, where Napoleon III and his army were captured. The incident marked the end of French hegemony in

Europe, and the beginning of German ascendancy. But the capture of France's leader did not lead to immediate defeat. In Paris, a Government of National Defence fought on for five months, while a hastily conscripted army lost a series of battles across northern France. Paris itself had fallen after a siege earlier in the year.

The city's troubles were far from over. Part of the treaty terms with the enemy allowed the Prussian army a brief, symbolic occupation of the city, amounting to a victory parade past resentful crowds of Parisians. A resistance organisation, originally intended to defend Paris against the enemy, prepared instead to fight for new causes – the chastisement of the government that had surrendered so readily, and the prevention of the return of the defeated Napoleon III. With most government officials hiding out in Versailles, the organisation took over, proclaiming the Paris Commune. Some of the soldiers sent to put down the uprising defected to its cause, leading the beleaguered government in Versailles to lean increasingly for troops on prisoners of war recently freed by the Germans.

The leading committee of the Paris Commune flew the red flag of Socialism in preference to the tricolour flag of the French Republic. It passed numerous progressive laws in areas such as labour reform, women's emancipation and the separation of church and state, but did so in a state of siege as troops loyal to Versailles began a counter-attack. Although loyal Communards manned the barricades in the streets, the Commune fell in late May 1871, amid ironic proclamations from the Versailles faction that the people of Paris were now free. Thousands died in the reprisals that followed, as mere association with the Commune was found to be cause for execution, imprisonment or transportation to New Caledonia in the South Pacific.

Saionji arrived in Paris shortly after the official inauguration of the Paris Commune, and found a city at war with itself. His prior experiences in Japan had left him with a respect for imperial France that was reflected in his letters home – as far as Saionji was concerned, this remained a scuffle between the government and 'rebels'. He attempted to begin his studies in a government stronghold where the teachers stashed firearms in the basement in case of an enemy attack. On an early tour of the city, he and his language tutor wandered into a firefight between rival factions, and his tutor was shot. When Saionji had left Japan, France had been a great power, ruled by an emperor, and with a powerful grip on its neighbours. By the time he arrived at his destination, the empire had fallen, and left-wing republicans had reduced Paris to a state of anarchy.

Saionji was astute enough to comprehend and combine the conflicting images he had seen of prosperity and poverty. *Europe will see a great revolution within ten years*, he wrote. *Recent European morals are too civilised and prosperous*. For Saionji, a product of Japan's aristocracy, and only in France at all because of its former military influence, the situation required: *a new Napoleon Bonaparte, a reactionary hero to maintain the status quo.*

Saionji's reactionary views, however, do not seem to

Saionji was not the only recent arrival from Japan. Jules Brunet (1838–1911) had been one of the French military advisers to the Shōgun Tokugawa Yoshinobu, who had 'disobeyed' orders by remaining in Japan after the Meiji Restoration. After fighting for the Shōgunate at the battles of Toba-Fushimi and Hakodate, he was evacuated on a French corvette and returned to France via Saigon. Back home, he was not tried for his alleged insubordination (which had been committed with the full knowledge of Napoleon III), and returned to active duty. Captured in the Franco-Prussian War, he was released in 1871, returning to Paris in time to play an instrumental role in the suppression of the Commune.

have been popular among his fellow Japanese students. He lamented that barely 1 per cent of his associates shared his stance, and fretted that the foreign studies experience, far from educating the next generation of Japanese statesmen, would only create a wave of revolutionaries. He was blunt and medieval in his opinions: *Anyone returning to Japan and advocating republicanism should be decapitated immediately as a warning to the others.*[9]

Giving up on the idea of Paris as the hub of a military superpower, Saionji soon moved to Switzerland, where learning French was safer, but in a colder climate. Preferring somewhere warmer, he fled in turn for Nice, which proved too expensive for him, leading to his removal again, this time to Marseilles. Here, it seems, his language studies began in earnest – he picked up a Marseilles accent that he never quite shook off.

When life in Paris finally returned to normal, Saionji returned there to continue his studies in both French and in law, eventually graduating with a law degree from the Sorbonne. Saionji was one of the success stories of the first great exodus from Japan of foreign students. His attitude, however, did not meet with the complete approval of his elders. In 1871, Iwakura Tomomi led a group of diplomats on a world tour to investigate state institutions in developed nations. The Iwakura Mission passed through Paris in 1872, where the young Saionji's ideas, by now somewhat more progressive and forcefully held, worried some of the party.[10]

He had picked up much of his ardour from his tutor Émile Acollas (1820–91), who had set up the Acollas Law School in 1871 for foreign students who wished to attend the University of Paris. Although Acollas was to become Saionji's greatest friend in France, he was also an unlikely, and, as the Iwakura

Mission began to guess, an unwelcome associate. In 1867, he had been a founder member of the League of Peace and Freedom, a revolutionary congress in Switzerland that had counted Giuseppe Garibaldi and Mikhail Bakunin among its attendees. Although dismissed by Karl Marx and the International Workingmen's Association, it was still a powerful force for revolution and republicanism, and Acollas, an avowed anti-monarchist, was one of its prime movers. While Saionji was in Switzerland, Acollas had been a lecturer at the University of Berne, only to hear that the Paris Commune had appointed him, *in absentia*, as dean of law at Paris University. He did not take up the post, but it was clear that French revolutionaries held him in high regard. Despite this, Saionji only spoke of his mentor with respect. *My teacher Emile Acollas had not a little power in the world of French political thought. Despite not possessing a wide and deep knowledge of the discipline, he was a savant and debater known for his great insights. Many radicals including [Georges] Clemenceau and [Charles] Floquet studied under him and I met them at his house several times.*[11]

By 1873, many of Saionji's fellow Japanese students in Europe and America had failed to perform to a satisfactory level and returned home.[12] Saionji stayed on in France, refusing further stipends from the government, but securing funds from new sources – quite possibly his younger brother, who had been adopted into the Sumitomo industrial combine, but also through the means of a part-time job at the Japanese legation in Paris. Saionji continued to study with Acollas, gaining a new Japanese classmate in Nakae Chōmin (1847–1901), a new student delivered by the Iwakura Mission as it continued on its way. Nakae studied alongside Saionji for two years, and on his return home would translate Rousseau's

Social Contract into Japanese. He also wrote of their tutor's beliefs in his later *Discourse by Three Drunkards on Government*, emphasising the moral nature of international law: 'Emile Acollas ... ranked international law in terms of morality rather than jurisprudence. According to Acollas ... [m] orality, unlike law, is made effective by the dictates of individual conscience. Similarly international law has no officials to enforce it, but depends instead only on the "consciences" of the nations involved.'[13]

After Nakae returned to Japan, Saionji witnessed Acollas' unsuccessful bid for a parliamentary seat in the 1876 French elections. Acollas stood on a platform that called for an amnesty for all involved in the Paris Commune, a federal, decentralised government, and a process of impeachment to aid in the removal of corrupt elected representatives. Although Acollas was unsuccessful in his political career, his acquaintance caused Saionji to meet many political luminaries of the day, including a young Georges Clemenceau, who was already a member of the municipal council, and would rise through the ranks as secretary, becoming president in 1875, before successfully running for the Chamber of Deputies in 1876.

It is easy to see how life in Paris would have appealed to Saionji. Photographs from the period show a dapper, floppy-haired man about town – a world removed from the expressionless, inscrutable statesman of later years. Clemenceau remembered Saionji as 'amiable' but 'impetuous'.[14] His biographers coyly mention 'a pretty woman of uncertain character' who was living with him at his Paris lodgings. They also report a degree of hellraising that shows Saionji had yet to shake off his rakish youth. In one incident, he was dining in a restaurant with his friend Kōmyōji Saburō, when Kōmyōji accidentally cracked a window. When a waiter demanded that they pay for the damage, Saionji did so, and then smashed the window in its entirety, proclaiming that it was now his to do with as he pleased.[15]

As one of a tiny handful of Japanese in Europe, Saionji was also an object of curiosity. A decade of open Japanese ports had led to a stream of European trading vessels returning from Japan with examples of Japanese culture. Reams of Japanese prints, cheap in their homeland but highly prized abroad, found their way onto the French art market. Meanwhile, the radical reforms of the Meiji government had driven many samurai families into poverty, forcing them to sell off their possessions – their furniture, porcelain and cloisonné enamels. All found their way to Europe on merchant ships making the return journey, encouraging a fad or trend for oriental artefacts.

The term *japonisme* was coined by Jules Claretie in *L'Art Français en 1872*. An 1862 exhibition in London of the collection of the former British ambassador Sir Rutherford Alcock helped popularise Japanese art in Europe, as did the use of many old Japanese books as packaging in consignments of porcelain. La Porte Chinoise, a store specialising in oriental goods, opened on the fashionable Parisian rue de Rivoli in the same year, with Parisian exhibitions focussed on Japanese interior design in 1867 and 1878. The subsequent fad for '*japonisme*' played a major part in the French arts in the late 19th century, and was an indirect influence on the Impressionists and Art Nouveau.

Japanese items were particularly popular, trading on the exoticism and mystery of a land that had ancient traditions in arts and crafts, yet was still 'new' to the outside world. But real Japanese visitors were in short supply, lending Saionji and Kōmyōji a unique appeal to the orientally-obsessed Parisians.

The two Japanese students made the acquaintance of the Paris literary set, largely through their association with Judith Gautier, the mistress of Victor Hugo. Herself the daughter of an author, Gautier had learned Chinese as a teenager, before an unhappy marriage to a much older man, Catulle Mendès. Separating from her husband in 1873, Gautier was the centre of circle of famous Parisian creatives, including Baudelaire, Flaubert, Gustav Doré and Edmond de Goncourt – a notorious collector of *japanneries*.

She was a friend of Richard Wagner, and a major proponent of oriental literature, publishing a collection of poetry translations, *Chinese Lyrics from the Book of Jade* (1867) and a novel, *The Imperial Dragon* (1869). Gautier traced her interest in the Orient back to a teenage encounter with two samurai in a London shopping arcade in 1862, during the International Exhibition. She remained fascinated by Japan, and latched on to Kōmyōji and Saionji as sources of inspiration. The young Japanese students were swiftly inducted into Gautier's clique, and dragged out on quaintly innocuous outings such as a day-trip on the roof of an open-topped omnibus. While wining and dining the Japanese, Gautier also picked their brains, and Saionji found his youthful interest in books put to unexpected uses. Gautier's next novel, *L'Usurpateur* (1875) ditched the Chinese themes in favour of a Japanese subject, a tale of forbidden love between the Emperor's consort and a dashing young Japanese nobleman, the Prince Nagato.[16]

Saionji also supposedly collaborated directly with Gautier on another project, relocating an old Chinese story into a more exotic Japanese setting. The result of their partnership did not appear until more than a decade later, with the premiere of Gautier's play *La Marchande de Sourires* (*The Seller of Smiles*) at the Odéon in Paris in 1888. Some might even see in the play an allegory of the confused civil strife in Saionji's homeland. The courtesan Rubyheart plots to ruin the marriage of her lover, Yamato (a poetic name for Japan itself). But

Yamato is not her true target; instead, she hopes to ensnare a man called Shimabara (named for the geisha quarter in Kyoto where Saionji once lived). The day is saved by an adopted son – perhaps an element here of autobiography.[17]

If the names were indeed poetic allusions to trouble at home, Saionji had every reason to make them. His work at the Japanese Legation introduced him to the uses to which diplomacy might be put. Far away from his native Japan, and seemingly out of touch with its intrigues and scandals, he was drawn back into civil strife by an unexpected route. Back in Japan, the Satsuma samurai Saigō Takamori began planning a new insurrection, hoping to do so with arms and ammunition purchased from foreign dealers. Unable to prevent French sellers from providing Saigō with guns on the open market, the Paris Legation instead fought back by outbidding his agents for the same guns.

The Satsuma Rebellion of 1877 was the unwitting result of the Meiji Restoration. Even some of the reformers among the old samurai class had not foreseen the Restoration's implications. In 1876, the Emperor had issued a proclamation banning the wearing of swords by all but military officers. In 1877, the old practice of paying samurai retainers in rice was stopped, leading to a backlash from former supporters of reform. Saigō Takamori, a Satsuma man who had formerly led Imperial forces during the civil war, turned on the order he had helped establish. A modern army, that he himself had helped to train, defeated his rebel forces. Behind the scenes, his military capacity had been diminished by the shrewd deals of the Japanese Legation in Paris.

After ten years in Paris, Saionji spoke fluent French, and might have been tempted to stay in France indefinitely. There was, after all, still work at the legation, and his associates were gaining great prominence. It is said that Acollas once asked Saionji if he intended to stay in France indefinitely – ten years had already passed, and an entire new generation of Japanese students were heading out into the world. Still headstrong,

Saionji replied: *He who would be a politician in my country cannot say what he thinks, cannot do what he says, has to be a hypocrite occasionally and tell lies. This is very distressing to me.*

Acollas supposedly answered: 'You are fortunate if in your country the politician can get along by lying occasionally. In my country, everything from top to bottom is a lie. There is no telling the truth, even occasionally.' [18]

If Saionji had forgotten the original purpose of his sojourn in France, events in the late 1870s jogged his memory. Even though Satsuma and Chōshū had been abolished, their influence lingered within factions that continued to jostle for prominence in Japan's new government. In 1880, Saionji and Kōmyōji boarded a ship for Japan, returning to their homeland after ten eventful years abroad. In many ways, the place to which they returned was unrecognisable.

5

The Eastern Liberal News

Saionji returned to a Japan without a feudal system. The samurai were gone forever, the last of their number co-opted into the modernised army and navy. The old class system had, at least in theory, been abolished with them. Where a youthful Saionji had once scandalised the court by suggesting he might marry a lower-class woman, marriage between the classes was now legally protected. The common people, outside the clan system, had been encouraged to adopt surnames for the first time, all the better to aid their identification in censuses and taxation. Commoners embraced this opportunity with gusto, although with humble lack of imagination, many of them selecting simple surnames containing vague geographical features, Field-Middle, Mountain-Base, Middle-Village, accounting for the myriad Tanakas, Yamamotos and Naka-muras of the modern Japanese telephone book.[1]

Technological changes were also readily apparent. A steam railway now linked Tokyo and Yokohama, and modern build-ings were sprouting from Tokyo construction sites. But behind the scenes, there were still signs that Japan remained mired in the past. Legendary claims for the Emperor's divine ancestry had led to the establishment of a Ministry of Gods, swiftly renamed the Ministry of Religion, which sought to inculcate acceptable levels of respect and loyalty in the Emperor's earthly subjects. Priests at Shinto shrines became government appointees, and were expected to teach the youth of their catchment area that the Emperor was himself a divine being.

For the students returning from abroad, Japan seemed to have lost its way. Reformers had petitioned the Emperor for the establishment of some sort of parliamentary democracy, perhaps initially with a form of limited suffrage for the property-owning classes. One of the petitioners was Saionji's old classmate Nakae Chōmin, who had become a figure in the Freedom and People's Rights Movement (*Jiyū Minken Undō*) – an extension of the teachings of Émile Acollas, unexpectedly springing up many thousands of miles from France. Nakae even introduced a new term into the Japanese language; he spoke of *minponshūgi*, literally 'an ideology rooted in the people' – the first local term for democracy.

Saionji's first activity on his return was to put his legal learning to use. He lectured in administrative law at the newly established Meiji Law School (later Meiji University), set up

Formerly an assistant law professor at the University of Grenoble, Gustave Emile Boissonade (1825–1910) had lectured Saionji and Japanese visitors in Paris in 1873 on the subjects of constitutional and criminal law. He was offered a three-year post as a government adviser in Japan, which was repeatedly extended for a total of 21 years. He taught at the Law School of the Ministry of Justice, and helped to draft much of Japan's new constitution and criminal code. His influence was damaged by the rise of the faction within the Japanese government that favoured a German legal model, but his contribution to the Japanese constitution was immense, and he became one of a handful of foreigners to be awarded the Order of the Rising Sun (2nd class).

by former students of the French legal expert Gustave Emile Boissonade.[2]

Law was not the only idea that Saionji had brought back with him from France. His experiences in Paris, and particularly with the young Clemenceau, had given him a healthy respect for the power of the press. Shortly before Saionji left France, Clemenceau had sought his advice on the title of a newspaper he planned on publishing. Perhaps with the rising sun in mind, Saionji had suggested *L'Aurore*. Clemenceau instead named his journal *La Justice*, and the first issue was published in January 1880. For the last few months of his Paris sojourn, Saionji had witnessed *La Justice* exerting a great influence on the path of left-wing politics in Paris – it was a lesson that neither he nor Clemenceau were to forget. Clemenceau would go on to write for a second paper in 1897, named *L'Aurore* as per Saionji's original suggestion – this was the paper that would eventually run the infamous 'J'Accuse' editorial by Emile Zola, regarding the Dreyfus Affair. Clemenceau quit *L'Aurore* in 1901 to 'edit' a weekly, *Le Bloc*, for which the bulk of the articles were Clemenceau's own work, and which helped establish him as a national force in French politics.

On Saionji's return to Japan, he found several of his former French studies colleagues were already grappling with the problems of Chōshū influence on the Japanese government, and had independently decided to begin their campaign of opposition by founding a newspaper. Saionji helped his friends canvas for money to fund the enterprise, and agreed to serve as its president and founding editor. Two thousand copies of the first issue were printed on 18 March 1881 – an eight-page broadsheet called the *Tōyō Jiyū Shinbun*, or *Eastern Liberal News*.[3]

Saionji's first editorial outlined his thoughts on the need for a level of administrative freedom ('political liberty'), which would in turn encourage a greater well-being and freedom of thought and action ('moral liberty') in the citizens of an enlightened state. It was a brave document in support of the movement to introduce free elections in Japan. The *Liberal News* was published daily, and continued to sell out its print-run (which stabilised at 1,600 copies a day), while Saionji, who had no recorded authorial experience beyond his alleged collaborations with Judith Gautier, struggled to come up with something to say in his daily editorials. *I thought it would be easy*, he wrote, *but once I started, my pen did not move as I wished. I then realised how difficult it was to be a journalist. [...] I did not do it to advocate people's rights or because I had a certain belief in the newspaper business. I just did it to please myself, but it became popular to my surprise. On some occasions, I must have exaggerated or denounced something, which fomented public discussion. After that, I became stubborn and jokingly said and did whatever the government was liable to dislike.*[4]

> On some occasions, I must have exaggerated or denounced something, which fomented public discussion. After that, I became stubborn and jokingly said and did whatever the government was liable to dislike.
>
> SAIONJI KINMOCHI

In fact, it is unclear how many of the editorials really were Saionji's work. His byline only appeared on the inaugural issue, and it is possible that he took the blame for later, unsigned articles because unlike his commoner associates, he was unlikely to attract severe punishment from his aristocratic peers. The paper's radical stance soon attracted the attention of the government, particularly Iwakura Tomomi, who attempted to persuade Saionji to give up his association with it. Other returnees had come back to Japan and taken posts in the government, an acceptable use of their foreign education; Saionji, on the other hand, risked becoming a pariah by returning home and, to some minds, opposing the very establishment that had sent him away to learn.

Saionji had struck a nerve. The power of the Satsuma and Chōshū oligarchs was waning within the government, while calls for an elected assembly from lesser officials were gaining ground. Not long before the publication of the first issue of the *Eastern Liberal News*, the Ministry of Domestic Affairs had been authorised to suppress the publication of seditious materials. Saionji's paper was not openly subversive, but still a great embarrassment to his relatives in government.

With Saionji still refusing to bow to pressure over the *Eastern Liberal News*, Iwakura resorted to blunter means of persuasion. He reported the matter to the Emperor himself, who responded with a secret Imperial command for Saionji to cease his association with the paper. The command was delivered by the Meiji Emperor's chamberlain, Tokudaiji Sanetsune – Saionji's own elder brother. Saionji responded by asking to plead his case before the Emperor in person, writing a memorial that set out his beliefs on the need for liberalisation of the Japanese political system. Since that was precisely the kind of airing of ideas that the government sought to discourage, his request was denied, and he had no choice but to resign his position.[5]

His departure created as much of a media stir as the *Eastern Liberal News* itself. Nakae Chōmin was unable to resist announcing that it was a matter of 'heavenly fate' in his next editorial – the characters for which also implied 'imperial will' in Japanese. A low-ranking employee of the magazine, Matsuzawa Kyūsaku, went even further, running off a printed bulletin on the incident, which not only exposed the Emperor's involvement, but also that Saionji had supposedly sworn not to disclose it to the paper's staff, and his silence had been bought with the offer of high-ranking positions in the civil service to some of his relatives. Matsuzawa and another staffer were briefly imprisoned, and Saionji was called in for questioning, but not punished further. At the very least, he had broken his promise by telling his associates why he was resigning – whether he was the unseen hand behind the allegedly independent actions of Matsuzawa is impossible to tell.

The case of the *Eastern Liberal News*, often glossed over in accounts of Saionji's life, is a fascinating precursor of his later diplomatic style. He had put his name to a single editorial and then probably delegated much of the later work to others. Such plausible deniability achieved two ends – allowing him to lend a ghostly support to the newspaper's articles, but also to shield the writers from the inevitable backlash. He gained secret concessions from the Emperor in return for his resignation, but then engineered an exposé of both the secret order and his own protest. Even with the sinking of the *Eastern Liberal News*, he had fostered great debate, and kept most of the staff out of trouble. The only fall-guys were Matsuzawa, who served 70 days in prison, and the distributor Ueda Chōjiro, who served 30 days.

The power and influence of noble patronage became clear shortly after his departure, when the newspaper tried a similar intrigue without a Saionji to shield it with a cosmetic resignation. Without his official consent, his colleague Matsuda Masahisa published an editorial that mourned Saionji's departure, only to claim that the ex-editor still supported the

Eastern Liberal News in spirit. Saionji's opponents pounced – either Matsuda was telling the truth, in which case Saionji was directly disobeying an imperial order by not severing all contact with the paper, or Matsuda was lying, in which case he was libelling a member of the nobility. Although such claims came to nothing, the insinuations and bad publicity were enough to make further publication too risky – the *Eastern Liberal News* suspended publishing on 30 April that year.

Had the incumbent administration stayed in power for much longer, the *Eastern Liberal News*, and Saionji, might have been entirely forgotten. Saionji's return to Japan, far from being a triumphant debut by a brilliant scholar of foreign studies, transformed in scant months into an igno-minious, embarrassing display of bravado. His activities, however, were soon regarded in hindsight as those of a brave and progressive statesman. The clique within the government opposing a national assembly was already losing ground, and gave way entirely that October after a failed power-play by an anti-Chōshū politician.

Loyalties within the post-Meiji government were often as confused as they had been during the Restoration. Although the factions had clashed over many issues, the final straw was the conclusion of a ten-year plan for the development of Japan's northernmost island, Hokkaidō. A public outcry arose over the plans of a clique of officials to buy out the resources of the abandoned development scheme at vast profit to themselves, leading the oligarch Ōkuma Shigenobu to counter by proposing the very elected assembly and con-stitution that the likes of Saionji had been calling for. Ōkuma was ousted by a rallying of the Satsuma and Chōshū nobles, who nevertheless offered their own support to the scheme in order to hang onto their proposals. By 12 October, an imperial edict announced that an elected assembly, the Diet, would be convened in 1890.

Overnight, liberals such as Saionji had transformed in the eyes of the establishment from troublemakers into progressive thinkers. As a noble with an avowed liberal streak, Saionji was particularly notorious, and soon approached by Itō Hirobumi, a Chōshū official, and offered an advisory position in the government.

Itō Hirobumi (1841–1909) had been one of the Chōshū Five, a group of young samurai from the rebellious domain who had flouted the Shōgun's authority by secretly leaving Japan in 1863. With the clandestine support of the Jardine-Matheson Company, they had been smuggled out of Yokohama disguised as English sailors – Itō and one of his companions had had to work as deckhands during the long trip from Shanghai to London. Returning in 1864 in a failed attempt to warn Chōshū not to attack foreign shipping in the Shimonoseki Strait, Itō was sent (officially this time) to study in America, and was one of the leaders of the Iwakura Mission in 1871. During the 1870s, while Saionji had been studying in France, Itō had occupied several government posts as a Chōshū oligarch, becoming chairman of the assembly of regional governors, and succeeding to the post of Minister for Domestic Affairs (Home Secretary) after the assassination of the previous incumbent.

Itō approached Saionji for his knowledge of legal issues, and, probably, for his family ties. As associate councillor, Saionji's job was to explain new legal and administrative proposals to government committees. Despite his progressive leanings, he was not known as a Satsuma-Chōshū sympathiser – perhaps Itō was hoping that the sight of Saionji explaining such proposals might lessen any potential opposition.

Although Itō appears to have kept Saionji out of critical power-broking meetings, Saionji's position as his right-hand man brought him into the administration – he was no longer an outsider publishing polemics, but a member of the government. Barely a year after commencing his associate position, he was invited to accompany Itō on a new fact-finding mission abroad.

This time, the issue was the Constitution. Its promulgation was no longer an issue – after all, an imperial decree had promised that one would be delivered by 1890. However, the nature of the constitution had yet to be determined. Boissonade could only advise so much – factions within the government still wanted to observe other states in action, particularly those administrations such as Britain and Belgium that combined parliamentary democracy with constitutional monarchy.

There were a dozen Japanese officials sent abroad with the Committee of Inquiry, and two hangers-on – Iwakura Tomomi having somehow added his son Tomosada to the ticket, with a sinecure post to investigate royal institutions. Of the party, only Saionji had spent a significant time abroad – even Itō had only studied in Britain for a year or so. As the party prepared to embark from Yokohama, Iwakura Tomomi himself came to say his farewells, not to his own son or even the nominal leader Itō, but to his long-term associate Saionji.

The itinerary of the Itō mission reflected the change in Japanese interests from the French precedents espoused by Boissonade, to a model that favoured Germany, the new rising power in Europe. They first went to Berlin, where they attended six months of lectures on constitutional law from Rudolf von Gneist, and then Vienna, where they listened to similar arguments from Lorenz von Stein. It was Berlin, however, that held sway – Gneist believed in the importance of limiting the power of parliament, in favour of increased power for a cabinet, which was sure to please Meiji oligarchs who wanted to maintain their authority. Gneist's student, Albert Mosse, met with the Committee of Inquiry and was instrumental in persuading them that the Prussian constitutional model would be better for Japan than that used in France or Britain. Mosse would later be invited to Japan on a three-year contract, where he would aid in the drafting of laws and local government mechanisms ahead of the promised parliamentary elections.

The Committee of Inquiry was away for 18 months, but was not the only group of Japanese officials in Europe at the time. To their chagrin, they heard that another investigative mission was touring Europe, in the form of Itagaki Taisuke, leader of the recently-formed Liberal Party. Itagaki was touring Europe at least in part with the blessing of the Japanese administration, but conspicuously displayed no interest in meeting with Itō's group. It was Saionji who travelled to Paris to meet with Itagaki, and brought him to Belgium to meet with the Committee of Inquiry – breaking the impasse and leading to later co-operation between the factions in government.

On his return to Japan, Saionji was promoted from Associate Councillor to Councillor, and moved to the Department of Legislation. He was also one of the beneficiaries of a new, modernised peerage that drew its nomenclature from ancient China, but owed a great deal to the Committee of Inquiry's reports on the European aristocracy. Feudalism might have been abolished in Japan, and the old lordly domains swept away, but the various faction members were awarded new titles in 1884 – in five ranks, Prince, Marquis, Count, Viscount and Baron. As the head (through adoption) of a leading noble family, Saionji was created a Marquis. This only served to increase his standing with the Chōshū clique – as the son of a commoner, Itō Hirobumi was lucky to be created a Count, and was now outranked once more, at least in protocol terms, by his protégé.[6]

Saionji was sent as Minister Extraordinary and Plenipotentiary to the court of the Austro-Hungarian Empire, serving another year outside Japan. As ever, he appears to have found an excuse to travel to Paris to catch up with old friends. 1885 saw the publication of *Poèmes de la Libellule* by Judith Gautier, which openly credited Saionji as her collaborator.[7]

His foreign experience, however, continued to stand him in good stead. Japan's nascent government remained a series of pushes and shoves between factions, many destined to become political parties. But external relations remained a crucial issue, particularly over the critical relationship between Japan and its interests in Korea.

Themselves humiliated by foreign powers, the Chinese were not about to back down to Japanese aggression. Although the Chinese general Li Hongzhang and Itō Hirobumi had agreed a form of non-intervention in Korean politics, the pro-Chinese Queen Min had already arranged for 2,000 Chinese 'military

> Institutions were not the only things that Japan hoped to copy from the West. The Meiji state also had colonial ambitions and had emulated Commodore Perry by using warships to force a treaty in 1876 opening Korean ports to Japanese trade. Korean officials were divided into two distinct factions, the pro-Japanese 'Progressives' and the pro-Chinese 'Sadae', whose rivalry culminated in a *putsch* on 4 December 1884 by Progressives with the support of guards from the local Japanese legation. The Chinese responded by sending in their own troops. The impasse was broken by a deal between Itō Hirobumi and the Chinese leader Li Hongzhang that would hold for a decade. The 'Convention of Tianjin' agreed that both would withdraw their troops, and would not re-enter Korea without notifying the other.

advisers' to be stationed in secret on Korean soil. Nor were the Chinese beneath shows of bravado. Two months after Saionji returned to Japan from Austria, the Chinese admiral Ding Ruchang put into port at Nagasaki to show off his two new battleships. Rowdy Chinese sailors clashed with the Nagasaki police, leading to swift calls within the government to upgrade Japan's own navy.

In November, Saionji accompanied Itō Hirobumi on a trip that was announced publicly as an inspection tour of the southern island of Kyūshū. In fact, the mission had an entirely different purpose, to head for the strategically important island of Tsushima, which sat midway between Korea and Japan. The island had long been coveted by foreign powers, and the Japanese had previously turned down requests, polite and not so polite, from both the British and the Russians. Saionji's mission had been occasioned by unsubstantiated rumours that the Russians were making moves on Tsushima once more, but, with no apparent sign of trouble, the party onboard the warship *Takao* decided to make a day-trip to Pusan, where they called on the very surprised, and somewhat nervous Japanese consul.[8]

Japan's new interest in the Prussian governmental model was to send Saionji to Germany. From December 1887 to August 1891, Saionji was back in Europe as an ambassador to the German Empire, to which Belgium appears to have been tacked on as an administrative afterthought. Although Paris was not part of his purview, he was there often enough that some Parisians appeared to assume that France was also his responsibility.

Just as a young Saionji had once arrived in France, and found it to be not quite the utopia of legend, he arrived in Germany in time to see its constitution stumbling. 1888 is remembered to this day by German schoolchildren with the mnemonic *'Drei achten, drei Kaiser'* – three eights, three emperors.

William I, the former King of Prussia and victor in the Franco-Prussian War who had become emperor of a united Germany in 1871, died in March 1888. His son and heir, Frederick III, outlived him by just 99 days; he had contracted inoperable cancer of the larynx. The death of Frederick III was an estimable loss to European politics. Much to the horror of his father's chancellor, Otto von Bismarck (1815–98), Frederick admired the political system presided over by his mother-in-law, Queen Victoria, and had hoped to introduce elements of the British system to Germany. Instead, he died on 15 June, leading to the disastrous reign of his son, Wilhelm II.

Wilhelm (1859–1941) was an arrogant youth, who had been sheltered from the harsh realities of military life. Whereas his grandfather had been a veteran of the Napoleonic Wars, and hoped to spare future generations such suffering, Wilhelm, or 'Kaiser Bill', soon clashed with Bismarck over foreign policy. Whereas Bismarck, in much the same style as Saionji, favoured careful diplomacy, the new emperor insisted that Germany deserved a 'place in the sun', and that achieving it would require a vigorous and aggressive foreign policy.

Saionji had to deal with the fall-out from the conflict between a young head of state and a much older, senior minister who enjoyed greater public popularity. It was an intriguing test of a state's constitution, and one that Saionji might have feared could occur in Japan at some future date. Saionji himself was able to deal with Bismarck without difficulty, concluding a treaty agreement in 1889 that reduced trade tariffs and, controversially for the Japanese, allowed for the possibility that Germans could be naturalised as Japanese citizens.[9]

He had less luck once the new Kaiser had taken over. Their sole recorded dialogue was a conversation in a theatre lobby in which the baffled ruler asked the diplomat how it was possible that the Japanese parliament building could burn down. Saionji replied, in all truthfulness, that it was made of wood. When it came to more important matters of state, the Kaiser and Bismarck were at such loggerheads that it was difficult to achieve much of substance.

Bismarck and the young Kaiser argued over matters of policy, particularly in regard to the Kaiser's right to appoint and dismiss ministers without consulting his chancellor, and Bismarck's dogged pursuit of anti-Socialist legislation. The most obvious sign came in the interference of the Imperial Household, Wilhelm's cronies, in the running of the Foreign Office, which was the domain of Bismarck. In one notable incident, Saionji and the other foreign ambassadors were invited to an eight o'clock banquet in celebration of the Kaiser's birthday. They were, however, invited by the Foreign Office. Whether by accident or by design, separate invitations soon arrived from the Imperial Household, requesting the presence of the diplomats for a night at the theatre, also beginning at eight. In this case, the Foreign Office was obliged to back down, shifting its banquet to the unsuitably early hour of five in the evening. Saionji observed at the time that the impasse, albeit a minor matter of diplomatic protocol, reminded him only too well of the posturing and conflicts between the old Japanese Imperial Household and its own 'foreign office', the Shōgunate.[10]

6

Japanism

Saionji came home once more on 21 August 1891, having spent 17 of the preceding 20 years abroad. He returned to a Japan with a constitution and with an elected assembly, the Diet. The political franchise, however, was very limited – only 1 per cent of the Japanese population, some 450,000 voters, were able to participate in the first elections, which restricted the franchise to adult men with a hefty property qualification. The Emperor retained the power of veto over his ministers' decisions.

The nature of power in the government was still difficult to define. Many of the old oligarchs were now serving politicians, enjoying greater power out of the cabinet than in it. By the time Saionji returned home, Japan was already on its fourth prime minister. Its first, his old friend Itō Hirobumi, had resigned his office in 1888 to head a new organisation, the Privy Council, originally intended to advise on the draft constitution. However, the Privy Council, as an unelected advisory body to the Emperor, soon gained a political clout that could often outweigh that of elected ministers. The incumbent ministry was largely composed of Satsuma men, a situation which left Itō and his allies with little to do but to bide their time for the next cycle of administration. On the resignation or end of term of the Satsuma clique, they were sure to be replaced by Chōshū men, which would bring Itō (and his protégé Saionji) back into office. Few early Japanese administrations lasted longer than 24 months, and there were plenty of events liable to force a resignation – Japanese politics was still dogged by political assaults and assassinations by radicals.

The crucial catalyst arrived, unexpectedly, from Russia shortly ahead of Saionji, and busied itself chasing girls. In what should have been a publicity coup for the incumbent administration, the heir to the Russian throne, Nicholas Alexandrovitch, had embarked on a round-the-world trip. After sailing from St Petersburg via the Suez Canal, he reached Japan in 1891 where he saw the sights, got a tattoo, and, his passions suitably aroused by reading Pierre Loti's *Madame Chrysanthème* en route, diligently pursued short-term sexual liaisons with local women. On 11 May, at the prominent lakeside resort of Ōtsu, Nicholas was attacked by one of his sword-wielding Japanese police escorts. The failed assassination attempt left him with a lifelong scar, and was the cause of deep international embarrassment to the Japanese.

The Meiji Emperor himself rushed to the Prince's bedside, and a Japanese woman committed suicide soon afterward, leaving a note that announced she hoped by her act to atone for national guilt. A slew of ministerial resignations in the aftermath irrevocably damaged the incumbent administration, and led to sweeping changes in the next election.[1] Nor was the incident forgotten in Russia. Over a decade later, the date of the assassination attempt was still marked in army and naval calendars, distributed to every military man in the

Tsar's service. The affronted Nicholas ensured that the occasion was literally marked in his soldiers' diaries.[2]

Saionji arrived just in time to take full advantage. After two years out of power, Itō Hirobumi was tasked with forming a new cabinet. Although he did not presume to give the inexperienced Saionji a job immediately, the newly returned nobleman was assigned a minor post in the new administration within two weeks of his arrival from Germany.

He spent an easy time living in borrowed accommodation in Tokyo, owned by his younger brother, who had been adopted into the rich Sumitomo family. With little to occupy him in his job, and the company of wealthy and powerful men, Saionji appears to have spent many evenings in 'tea-houses' and restaurants with his friends. Whether this was a change in his behaviour, or simply an extension of the lifestyle he had been living in Europe, it is difficult to determine – there is certainly much more *evidence* of his carousing once he returned to Japan, but he was often in the company of Itō, whose nocturnal activities were always a source of great excitement to the Japanese press.

With French as the everyday language of the Russian aristocracy, it is unsurprising that Prince Nicholas was reading *Madame Chrysanthème* on the voyage to Japan. Published in 1887 by Pierre Loti (1850–1923) the novel was the height of the *japonisme* that had been stirred in part by Judith Gautier. An account of a 'temporary marriage' between a foreigner and a courtesan in Nagasaki, it was a major influence upon Puccini's opera *Madama Butterfly* (1903). In the early 20th century, Loti would follow in Saionji's footsteps by collaborating directly with Gautier on the Chinese-themed play *Daughter of Heaven* (1911).

Drinking and whoring in the brothel quarter was not an unusual activity for wealthy men from the old families, but it was often at odds with Japan's rush towards modernisation. The new police force, often known in poetic slang as the Eight

Winds, had an avowed interest in maintaining public morals, leading to a series of police raids on houses of 'ill-repute'. On several occasions, Itō and Saionji were among the clientele, leading to a great deal of discomfiture, not necessarily for the clients, but for the police who were then obliged to back off.

Traditionally, clients of the geisha houses used pseudonyms to preserve their anonymity. Saionji was usually known as Mr Ōtera – 'Honourable Temple', the temple being the *ji* of his real name. However, his presence at the geisha houses became unexpectedly infamous when a song he penned in a whimsical moment was adopted as an unofficial partygoers' anthem. It contained a reference to the elements, intended as a playful dig at the activities of the police force, and was never intended for public distribution. Unfortunately for him, it was soon set to music and became a regular feature of geisha-house per-formances in two districts. Almost impenetrably obtuse, its lines were nevertheless rather racy by the standards of the day, suggesting that it was uncouth for the 'wind' to interfere in what went on behind closed doors, in the pokey 'four-mat room' of a brothel.

> *The wind and malice rustle*
> *The hare-foot-fern that hangs from the eaves*
> *Of the assignation hall.*
> *Even does its gentle rustle*
> *In room of four mats and a hall*
> *To this or that the attention call.*[3]

Saionji, however, may have been unfairly tarred with the same brush as Itō, simply because of the popularity of his song. He had other reasons for his visits to the geisha quarter, as he was resuming a long relationship with a prominent entertainer, Okiku, who went by the stage-name Tamah-achi. She was allegedly from a samurai family, but had fallen on hard times after her relatives had backed the Shōgunate during the Meiji Restoration.[4] The couple had known each other since before Saionji left for Paris as a student, and their relationship resumed on his permanent return. Okiku had given birth to Saionji's daughter, Shinko, sometime around 1884.

Saionji's high noble rank was to prove to be another advantage. Itō's new government struggled with the same problems as its predecessor, as well as a hostile Diet. Itō himself was injured when his rickshaw crashed into a coach carrying an Imperial princess. But Itō was at least assured of some support from the nobility, particularly after he installed Saionji as Vice-President of the House of Peers in November 1893. Like Saionji's ancestors, the manipulative Fujiwara clan, Itō may have hoped to steer decisions by appointing his own protégé to a supposedly superior position. In May 1894, Saionji gained a new accolade when he was appointed as the newest member of the Privy Council.

Despite a series of posts that had nothing to do with diplomacy, Saionji's experience of foreign relations was soon put to the test once more. A series of events, initially seemingly unconnected, began to demonstrate that China was once more supporting anti-Japanese factions in Korea, in contravention of the Convention of Tianjin.

In 1893, the Korean would-be revolutionary Kim Ok-gyun was assassinated on his way to a meeting in Shanghai. His body was sent back to Korea, where it was mutilated and put on display to discourage other 'rebels' – Kim's policy had been broadly pro-Japanese, and his treatment was widely seen as an insult to the Japanese.

Matters worsened in 1894 when the Korean Donghak movement, a peasant organisation that had been in existence for many decades, blossomed into a revolutionary movement. An uprising of farmers against landlords characterised the ruling class as toadies and cronies of the Japanese – rich, progressive Koreans had been sending their children to Japanese schools, which only accentuated the backlash. Fatefully, the Korean government asked for Chinese military aid in putting down the uprising. The Chinese obliged with 3,000 troops. Under the terms of the Convention of Tianjin, such an act required them to 'notify' the Japanese. This they duly did, although as soon as the Convention was put to the test in this manner, the sides turned out to disagree on the meaning of the word. The Japanese protested that 'notification' implied consultation and approval, which they firmly withheld.

Claiming that the Chinese had violated the Convention, at the very least in spirit, the Japanese sent their own troops into Korea, leading to two foreign powers on Korean soil, both ostensibly there to put down a local revolt. The Chinese soon left, but the Japanese remained, seizing control of the capital Seoul and installing a new pro-Japanese government.

Although Japan already had an ambassador in Seoul, Saionji was sent to reassure the Korean ruler of the Japanese Emperor's good intentions. His mission achieved limited success. He met with both the nominal king Gojong and with the king's powerful father, the Daewon-gun. As in Saionji's native Japan, there was some confusion as to who precisely was in charge – the king, the father who had acted as his regent throughout his youth, or the family of Queen Min, one of the king's pushier wives. The Daewon-gun, an amateur artist in his spare time, charmed Saionji by presenting him with scroll-paintings of some orchids in his own hand. He also scandalised him by demonstrating a complete disinterest in the very modernisation that the Japanese hoped to encourage. When Saionji suggested to the Daewon-gun that a railway network and modern industries would help Korea stand its ground against foreign aggression, the Daewon-gun supposedly replied that railways required the levelling of mountains and filling of valleys, itself an act tantamount to breaking the spine of a state. Saionji thought it to be a ludicrous opinion, and in later life would relate the anecdote to demonstrate the folly of 'traditional' beliefs.[5] The situation in Korea soon broke out into open war between China and Japan, but Saionji had little direct involvement. After his fruitless mission to Seoul, he returned to Tokyo to take up a post within Itō's cabinet, as Minister of Education.

His encounter with the Daewon-gun still heavy in his thoughts, he was soon embroiled in a struggle with the conservative educational community. Saionji pushed for modern education, against school principals who favoured traditional values – both the classical, Confucian education promoted by Saionji's predecessor in the past, and the 'Emperor-worship' promoted by the Ministry of Religion. Saionji was publicly accused of being 'cosmopolitan' – the term intended pejoratively to describe someone who wilfully jettisoned traditional values for no real gain. It was an irritating time for Saionji, but as has happened so often in his career, his preoccupation with other matters kept him away from a scandal that would probably have otherwise ended his career.

While Saionji was quarrelling with school boards, his associate Mutsu Munemitsu (1844–97) was busy on diplomatic matters, in the post of Foreign Minister. Paramount among these was the negotiation of a peace treaty at the end of the Sino-Japanese War. The Japanese advance into Korea had surpassed all expectations; by the time the Chinese sued for peace in spring 1895, Japanese troops had pushed their enemies out of Korea, crossed the Yalu River into China, and successfully occupied the Liaodong Peninsula. Liaodong was not merely a valuable piece of real estate – it also commanded one side of the sea route towards Beijing's port of Tianjin. A navy in control of Liaodong possessed the power to blockade the sea-route to the Chinese capital, rendering the area of crucial significance. Meanwhile, far to the south, the Japanese had also seized Taiwan (Formosa), the large island that sat at the end of the Ryūkyū chain, along with the nearby Pescadores Islands, a strategically important harbour.

Saionji and Mutsu were not only linked through their association with foreign diplomacy. They were also part of a group that published a 'cosmopolitan' magazine in 1896, under a name chosen by Saionji himself: *Japan in the World* (*Sekai no Nippon*). The magazine was intended as an answer to the blinkered nationalism and Pan-Asian propaganda of other recent journals.

Territorial gain was top of the Japanese agenda. Li Hongzhang made several attempts to negotiate through diplomatic channels, only to be rebuffed by Itō Hirobumi. The advance stalled through the winter of 1894–5, and Li wisely made stronger overtures in January in order to prevent the Japanese military machine gearing up for a springtime assault on Beijing itself. The delay until January led to one final Japanese victory, at the vital harbour of Weihaiwei – the other side of the strait commanding the Tianjin sea-route.

A humiliated Li Hongzhang arrived in Shimonoseki to negotiate terms. To add injury to insult, he was assaulted and wounded by a Japanese man on his way to his lodgings. It was another embarrassing incident like that of the assault on Prince Nicholas four years earlier; Japanese public reaction was contrite and apologetic, but not quite so much as in the earlier scandal – it was, after all, unlikely that the Chinese would retaliate. However, a physical attack on a foreign diplomat, amid critical negotiations for a peace treaty, was unlikely to improve Japan's international standing.

Saionji presided over the treaty negotiations. Not even the Japanese imperialists could agree fully on the terms – some were opposed to outright colonial activities in China, for fear that foreign capital and cheap labour would encourage an industry that might compete all too well with Japan's own. However, there were enough hawks in the cabinet for Japan's terms to take a predictable shape. The cabinet approved a draft treaty comprising 40 articles, almost exclusively lifted from a stack of pre-existing treaties between European powers and China. The Chinese countered with a series of rewordings and deletions – they were, it was clear, determined to prevent the Japanese from enjoying similar advantages to the white races already carving China up.

The sticking-point was the issue of reciprocity. Japan demanded and received Most Favoured Nation status – the chance to benefit from the terms of any treaties that China concluded with other powers. But China wanted the deal to go both ways: if Japanese citizens were to enjoy trade privileges, travel concessions and extraterritorial rights in China, surely the Chinese should enjoy the same in Japan?

Saionji would not listen. The Japanese refused, he said, *to be placed in their relations with China in a more disadvantageous position than the European powers.*[6] As far as Saionji was concerned, the imposition of an Unequal Treaty on the Chinese was not aimed at annoying the Chinese; he was keen to stress that it was there to promote intercourse with China, but only *in* China, and not in Japan. More importantly for

Saionji's Eurocentric perspective, it would help to establish Japan as worthy of consideration on an equal footing with the European powers. To Saionji, China was already falling apart, but in joining in the fight over resources, he might save Japan from a similar fate.

Li Hongzhang had little room for compromise. When he protested at severe Japanese terms, he was informed that over 60 warships were ready to steam for Tianjin, there to land troops for an attack on Beijing itself. On 17 April, he signed a crushing treaty, promising Liaodong, Taiwan and the Pescadores to Japan, along with an indemnity of 200 million taels (an amount of silver worth perhaps £1.7 billion in 2008 currency). In addition, China was obliged to open four ports to Japanese traders, and to grant Japan the coveted Most Favoured Nation status that would allow it to benefit from any treaties signed with other (i.e. Western) powers.

The Meiji Emperor issued a proclamation that carefully avoided gloating over the Chinese defeat, while the Japanese population celebrated. It was as if Japan had been admitted to a special club, granted membership of the group of imperialist nations that were already exploiting China for their own ends. A scant 40 years after the arrival of Commodore Perry and his Black Ships, the Japanese were imposing 'unequal treaties' of their own, and on no less a victim than China itself.

The elation lasted less than a fortnight, before Japan was delivered a sharp wake-up call. In what would become known as the Triple Intervention, representatives arrived from Russia, Germany and France. Diplomatic issues elsewhere had led to the triple embassy, but most of the impetus came from Russia. The new Tsar, not yet even crowned, was Nicholas II, that same Nicholas who had experienced Japanese hospitality first-hand in Ōtsu when a policeman had tried to kill him. Despite the later efforts of the Japanese to put him at his ease, and cordial communiqués with the Meiji Emperor, Nicholas never quite forgave the Japanese.

Count Sergei Witte, one of the Tsar's ministers in St Petersburg, observed: 'It seems to me that the attack left [Nicholas] with an attitude of hostility toward and contempt for the Japanese ... an unpleasant, contemptible and powerless people who could be destroyed at one blow from the Russian giant.'[7] The Tsar was not concerned with the Japanese seizure of Taiwan – it was a south-sea issue and not really of interest to Russia. He was far more worried about the idea of a Japanese presence on the Liaodong peninsula, threatening Russian interests in north China, particularly regarding southward extensions of the Trans-Siberian railway. It also walled Korea in between Japan and a Japanese possession, making a mockery of the nation's supposed independence.

The triple embassy politely requested that the Japanese clear out of Liaodong, and Itō had little choice but to agree. The Japanese islands were virtually undefended, with most of the empire's military forces recuperating in China and Taiwan. Not wishing to call the bluff of the new Tsar, Itō agreed, and pulled the Japanese out of Liaodong. He demanded an additional indemnity, but it was still a grave humiliation for the Japanese.

Mutsu Munemitsu, the Foreign Minister, had been happy to take the credit for negotiations when the Chinese were agreeing to everything. As the Treaty of Shimonoseki fell apart, he now took much of the blame. But throughout the time of the Triple Intervention, Mutsu was on sick leave. He had fallen from a boat in Hiroshima, aggravating his already chronic tuberculosis. He was replaced by a minister who had prior experience of dealing with French and Germans, and whose French was up to the challenge of dealing with aristocratic Russians – Saionji Kinmochi.

As acting Foreign Minister, Saionji was party to the negotiations and arguments, without ever being associated with their ignominious conclusion. He is likely to have been relieved at this, as he would never have counselled such a foolhardy series of demands in the first place.

As Education Minister, he had already complained that the attitudes of the Japanese school system seemed geared towards the creation of a belligerent nation: *There is a great insistence on 'Japanism' and an 'aggressive fighting spirit', but behind these are lies and greed. There will be no end to the misery which arose without warning from victory in the war, unless we develop adequate countermeasures.*[8]

> There is a great insistence on 'Japanism' and an 'aggressive fighting spirit' … There will be no end to the misery which arose without warning from victory in the war, unless we develop adequate countermeasures.
>
> SAIONJI KINMOCHI

The 'Japanism' to which Saionji refers was not the artistic trendiness of his old friends in the Parisian literary set. Instead, it was a dangerous doctrine of manifest destiny, promoting the Japanese as the rightful rulers of Asia. It was widely believed, and with some justification, that Japan's humiliation had been caused by excessive demands, in contravention of the unwritten rules regarding proportional response and reasonable diplomacy. The German ambassador had actually stated as much, in a momentary outburst during the Triple Intervention negotiations – a worrying insinuation that Japan still had much to learn before it was truly allowed into the circle of Great Powers.

Chided for biting off more than he could chew, Mutsu tendered his resignation from his sick-bed in May 1896. Saionji, who had been doing his job for the previous year, was officially made Foreign Minister in his stead. Once in his new job, Saionji tried to smooth things over with the Russians by sending a high-profile delegation to the new Tsar's coronation, and instructing them to remain on their best behaviour. *In view of the special circumstances in which Japan finds herself in regard to Russia*, Saionji wrote with impressive understatement, *the Japanese must first consider profiting from the exceptional occasion of the Coronation.*[9] But if he hoped to allay Russian fears, he would be disappointed.

7

The Yellow Peril

Saionji's career as Foreign Minister was short-lived. The Itō cabinet was out of office again by 31 August 1896, replaced once more by a Satsuma faction. By pure, unadulterated luck, the handover of power allowed Saionji to escape any association with a terrible incident a few weeks later in Korea.

It is sure to have had nothing to do with him – it demonstrated precisely the arrogance and belligerence against which he had been warning for some time. The new Japanese ambassador in Korea, Miura Gorō, was a reluctant appointee, a military man nevertheless determined to maintain Japan's hold on Korea after the embarrassment of the Triple Intervention. He did so by forming an uneasy alliance with the Daewongun, the father of the incumbent King Gojong, but remained curiously inactive in diplomatic matters. Instead, he stayed at the Japanese Legation and made a show of copying out Buddhist sutras – a harmless hobby, at which he announced he intended to persevere until such time as King Gojong required his services. Such false piety hid Miura's true intent, a bold scheme for a *coup d'état*.

Japan and the Daewon-gun believed themselves to have

a common enemy in Queen Min, the chief wife of King Gojong. Her friendships with the Chinese had been a contributing factor towards the previous unrest in Korea, and now she seemed to be developing an alliance with the Russians. Miura planned to use the Training Unit, an 800-strong battalion of Japanese-trained Koreans, as the main agents of his coup, seizing control of the palace in the name of the Daewon-gun. Apparently, he had not told the Daewon-gun of his whole plan, which was to blame the entire mess on Korean nationals, and then to call in Japanese military 'aid' at what would obviously be a time of national strife.

The Daewon-gun thought he was agreeing to something far less draconian – a position for himself as a figurehead, some pro-Japanese appointments, and the politically-charged decision to send his grandson, the future king of Korea, to Japan as a student for three years. Nor did he expect the conspirators to rush into action so swiftly. Determined to purge pro-Japanese influences from the capital, Queen Min prevailed upon her husband to disband the Training Unit, forcing Miura to move his plans forward.

The Daewon-gun was dragged from his bed in the small hours of 8 October 1895, and accompanied the conspirators to the palace. En route, he seems to have had some presentiment of trouble, at one point refusing to go any further until the Japanese assured him that they were not planning on killing his son the King. The main rebels, Japanese civilian ex-pats recruited by one of Miura's agents, promised him that the King would be safe – a careful choice of words, since they had already been instructed to find and kill Queen Min.

Some 30 Japanese barged into the sleeping palace, brandishing swords and threatening the occupants at gunpoint, demanding to know where the Queen was. It would have been somewhere around this point that they realised nobody knew what the Queen actually looked like. Meeting with loyal silence, they killed three ladies-in-waiting before finding a woman of regal bearing hiding beneath some bedclothes. Correctly surmising that this was Queen Min, they dragged her out by the hair and beheaded her, before pouring kerosene onto her corpse in the courtyard and setting it ablaze in an attempt to conceal the evidence.[1]

Amazingly, Miura hoped to cover up as much of the incident as possible, clamping down on Seoul's telegraph network, and shutting down palace communications. The palace's so-called Self-Defence Force was unarmed and presented little opposition, but its supervising officer was an American, William M Dye, who refused to leave and who the Japanese dared not harm. It was Dye who passed on the news to other foreigners, and the story reached the outside world within a week.

Although Miura had been hired by Itō's administration and, in fact, had been recommended by Itō himself, it was Itō's successor who had to deal with the political fall-out. The conspirators were rounded up and shipped to Japan for a trial, which was soon called to a halt through lack of evidence. The conspirators went unpunished, although transcripts revealed what was already suspected, that the attempted coup and murder of the Queen had been entirely instigated by Japanese agents. In the aftermath of the cover-up, far from increasing Japanese influence in Korea, Miura's blunder had sunk it to an all-time low. Possibly to Japan's great future misfortune, one of the foreigners present in Seoul at the time was the 30-year-old Stephen Bonsal – 24 years later, as a major with the American delegation at the Paris Peace Conference, Bonsal would remember the incident, and allowed it to colour much of his attitude towards the Japanese: 'Despite the fact, the undoubted fact, that the Imperial Japanese minister, General Miura, instigated the murder of the Min Queen … and the undeniable fact that his clerks … led the assassins who cut her to pieces, many think that I take a too extreme view of the situation, and certainly an impractical one. She was a gallant little woman who would not be bullied or even browbeaten, and so the Japanese murdered her. She may not have been the only "man" in Korea, as many disgusted for-eigners at the time asserted, but she was an outstanding one and put to shame the chicken-hearted king, her husband.'[2]

In February the following year, an understandably angry King Gojong escaped his palace confinement and took refuge at the Russian legation. From there, he disbanded his pro-Japanese cabinet. Russian influence in Korea was now on the rise, and the Tsar continued to capitalise on the gains made through the Triple Intervention, and the continued antipathy towards Japan in Korea. By 1898, the Russians seized conces-sions in Liaodong for themselves, gaining a 25-year lease on the strategic Port Arthur, and immediately commencing con-struction of tracks to link it with the Trans-Siberian railway. Soon afterwards, the British would insist on a port of their own to 'balance' the Russian presence – they were permitted to rent Weihaiwei ('Port Edward') from the Chinese for the dura-tion of the Russian presence on the other side of the strait.

Throughout this time, Saionji and Itō maintained a low profile – Saionji's one conspicuous act being the issuing of a direct order to one of the transgressors to return home to face trial.[3] Saionji himself returned to Paris, where an attack of acute appendicitis compromised his plans to catch up with old friends. Itō made his own way to Europe, ostensibly to attend the jubilee celebrations for Queen Victoria, although he met up with the convalescing Saionji in Paris, and the two men held meetings with the French Foreign Minister, Gabriel Hanotaux.

There were already signs that, far from entering the international community with the Sino-Japanese War, Japan was being excluded from it. Hanotaux had engineered a rapprochement with the Tsar, which left the Japanese without French support. Meanwhile, the British had offered vague commiserations to the Japanese over the Russian actions in Korea, but no concrete support – Gojong was, after all, the sovereign of Korea, and he had fled to the Russian legation of his own free will.[4]

Back in Japan, Saionji settled in a new house, clearly with the expectation that Itō would be back in office soon. He composed a poem, part of which alluded to Cao Cao, a wily politician from the *Romance of the Three Kingdoms*:

On summer days I read my books
In winter I go hunting
The heart's desire of Cao is not
For great achievements yet.

A reader familiar with the Chinese classics would be expected to remember the original context of Cao's claim to like reading and hunting: that despite such interests, 'I am but an ignoramus who began life with a simple bachelor's degree and recommendations for filial devotion. And when the troubles began, I built for myself a little cottage in the country near Qiao, where I could study in spring and summer and spend the rest of the year in hunting till the empire was once more tranquil and I could emerge and take office.'[5]

Saionji's opportunity for action presented itself on

Christmas Day 1897, with the collapse of a coalition cabinet. Itō Hirobumi was invited to form a new administration, and soon asked Saionji to return to office once more as the Minister for Education. Saionji did so, with a controversial attitude that restated the beliefs in moral education that he had inherited from Émile Acollas and previously mentioned in *Eastern Liberal News* editorials. Saionji argued that ... *at present, not only the organization of the educational system was bad, but the educational atmosphere was bad, and therefore the right educational atmosphere should be created first of all.*[6]

Dangerously for a man of his class, Saionji's complaint struck at the very heart of Japanese culture. He complained that Japanese social interactions, and hence Japanese society as a whole, were still rooted in the etiquette of the samurai era, which 'consisted merely of the rules for looking up and looking down'. Japanese society lacked any mechanism for true dialogue, debate or contention, and instead comprised those who gave orders and those who obeyed. Ironically, even though he was an aristocrat and used to being obeyed, his complaints were largely ignored.

Subtle but powerful reforms were introduced in the next government, that of Yamagata Aritomo which was in power from 1898 to 1900. Yamagata introduced a rule that only serving officers could hold the post of army or navy minister – ensuring that the cabinet would always be forced to listen to military concerns. As ever, there were confused loyalties – Yamagata interpreted his role as one of preserving the imperial institution by keeping political parties, the Diet and democracy at arm's length. Yamagata, and later his protégé Katsura Tarō, would become the chief rivals to Saionji and Itō Hirobumi, and the two factions would alternate in power for the first decade of the 20th century.

Yamagata's second term as Prime Minister coincided with the Boxer Rebellion in China, and Japanese troops played a major role in the relief of the foreign legations in Beijing – a role played up by the Japanese press, which noted that Lieutenant-General Yamaguchi Motoomi was the highest-ranking officer in the multinational relief force, and that hence Japan was 'leading' the rest of the world. Foreign powers, however, had also noted it, leading to the swift dispatch of a German field marshal to take over, to prevent the relief force from being led by an Asiatic.

Prime Minister Yamagata resigned soon after the end of the Boxer Crisis, ostensibly to hand over to Itō Hirobumi, but actually in a deliberate attempt to dump leadership in Itō's hands before he was properly organised. Itō had recently formed a new political party, and Yamagata's exit from office seemed intended to thrust authority on the new organisation before it was properly ready.

Saionji was one of the first men to join Itō's *Rikken Seiyūkai* (Friends of Constitutional Government), which was fated to become the most powerful party in Japanese politics for a generation. Barely a month after the *Seiyūkai*'s official formation, Itō was asked to form a government, which immediately faced heavy opposition from allies of Yamagata in the House of Peers. Saionji briefly served as Acting Prime Minister when Itō fell ill, but soon resigned once more in favour of his mentor. Faced with insurmountable opposition to tax reforms and a new budget, Itō resigned after only a few months. It was traditional for a Prime Minister's entire cabinet to resign with him, but in an unprecedented move, the thwarted Finance Minister Watanabe Chiaki refused to do so. The Emperor was thus obliged to appoint a new Acting Prime Minister, and Saionji served briefly in this role a second time from 10 May to 2 June 1901. His role in office was largely to dismiss the errant Finance Minister and tidy up party affairs before the inevitable new administration formed by his rival, Yamagata's protégé Katsura Tarō.

Saionji, however, was still able to attend cabinet meetings in his function as Privy Councillor, forming an important conduit between the incumbent administration and his own party. By 1903, Saionji had been appointed the head of the *Seiyūkai* at Itō's insistence, giving the opposition party an occasionally unwelcome voice in Katsura's administration. *Itō told me to take it*, wrote Saionji of the position, *and it was more or less a case of my giving it a try to see if I could be of any use.*[7]

Katsura, a military man and former Minister of War, handed out large numbers of decorations or court ranks to prominent businessmen and military sympathisers, and petitioned the Emperor to award the highest honours to anti-democrats such as Yamagata Aritomo. His first term as Prime Minister, which lasted an impressive four and a half years, saw the Anglo-Japanese Alliance, a treaty that had been brewing ever since Britain had refused to join the Triple Intervention in 1895. The alliance, which would last in some form or other until 1923, was based in part on the belief that the plucky Japanese, now widely known for their participation in the relief of the Legations during the Boxer Rebellion, were the 'British of Asia' – an island empire with a strong martial reputation. The treaty allowed that either nation would declare itself neutral if the other went to war with a third party. If war broke out with more than one enemy, then the other party would enter that war on its ally's side. The wording was designed by the British as a gentle admonition to Russia to curb its expansion in Manchuria and East Asia, but was regarded by the Japanese as more of an encouragement – a guarantee, of sorts, that Britain would not interfere if Japan went to war with Russia, and a promise of assistance if Russia called on any other nation for assistance against Japan.

Saionji gave a strongly-worded speech in November 1903, in which he warned his countrymen that Japan was still in a transitional period towards true parliamentary democracy, and cautioned against belligerent policies abroad.

> **I am not worried about any lack of patriotism but afraid of where an abundance of patriotism will lead us.**
>
> SAIONJI KINMOCHI

We will not win the respect and sympathy of other nations if we are hot headed and discourteous – a source of weakness even in times of peace, but especially in times of trouble … I am not worried about any lack of patriotism but afraid of where an abundance of patriotism will lead us. We must avoid infantile demonstrations which will weaken the country.[8]

Nevertheless, on 8 February 1904 Japan went to war against Russia. Notoriously, the official declaration of war arrived three hours after the Japanese navy had commenced hostilities with an attack on the Russian East Asia Fleet. Tsar Nicholas II rushed into retaliation, and much to the surprise of many, including many Japanese politicians, the Japanese armed forces delivered a crushing defeat on the Russians.

The Russo-Japanese War ended with a resounding Japanese victory. Troubled by the first stirrings of revolution at home, the Tsar eagerly accepted the mediation of the US President Theodore Roosevelt. So, too, did Katsura, whose war effort risked bankrupting Japan if hostilities continued for much longer. Negotiations concluded with the Treaty of

Portsmouth, for which Roosevelt would receive the Nobel Peace Prize.

The terms allowed that both Japan and Russia would quit Manchuria and restore it to China. In return, Japan would receive the southern part of Sakhalin Island just north of Hokkaidō, valuable territory on China's Liaodong Peninsula, as well as the right to operate the southern part of the Manchurian railway. The preceding Taft-Katsura Agreement allowed that the US would not challenge Japanese sovereignty in Korea, transforming it into a Japanese colony.

The gains for Japan were superb, not the least in Saionji's preferred field of international diplomacy. In defeating Russia and acquiescing to American mediation, Japan was adjudged worthy of status as a 'first-class' nation. Japan's representatives abroad were no longer 'Ministers', speaking with the authority of the Japanese Foreign Minister, but 'Ambassadors', speaking with the authority of the Japanese head of state.[9] The improvement in Japan's international standing, however, was largely lost on the population, which had been led to believe that they would get much more from the victory. In precisely the sort of 'infantile demonstrations' that Saionji had warned against, two days of rioting broke out in Tokyo, Kobe and Yokohama, with 17 reported deaths and considerable damage to property. At the riots, and at hundreds of subsequent rallies and protests in the ensuing weeks, the Japanese renounced the terms of Portsmouth, regarding it as a betrayal. The Japanese people, it was argued, wanted *all* of Sakhalin, not just the southern part; *all* of Liaodong, not just pieces of it. It was widely believed, that, in being asked to fall back from many newly acquired territories, Japan was being treated in the treaty negotiations like a defeated power, and not the victor. It was a sign of an increasingly widespread sense of entitlement that would only be exacerbated in years to come by the free rein afforded the Japanese in East Asia by the collapse of Tsarist Russia and the continuing Anglo-Japanese Alliance.

Even though Katsura had been Japan's leader in the unprecedented victory over Russia, his ministry was dealt a deathblow by the unrest over the Treaty of Portsmouth. In early 1906, Katsura threatened to resign, and made official overtures to Saionji, offering him the opportunity to form a new government. The move seems to have been intended as a bluff – since Saionji had twice declined to form a cabinet in the past, Katsura was hoping that he would refuse again, 'forcing' Katsura to remain in office, but also obliging Saionji to offer him the support of the *Seiyūkai* for the remainder of his term.

Instead Saionji surprised Katsura by agreeing to the offer. *I shall not be slow*, he said, *to take the duty upon myself and grapple with the difficult situation – and this not for the sake of the* Seiyūkai *but to settle the minds of the people and stabilize the State.*[10]

Saionji was true to his word, beginning his first official term as Prime Minister by issuing a controversial speech in defence of the Treaty of Portsmouth. Against the advice of his colleagues, he even had the speech published in a Tokyo newspaper, to make sure everyone got the message. He sternly told the Japanese that his own position was *one of jubilation at the return to peace*, but added:

However, we should also appreciate the peculiar character of this [Portsmouth] Peace Conference which, called on the advice of the President of the United States of America, is an attempt to secure negotiations for peace between Japan and Russia as equal states. This is very different from the situation

*where a defeated nation sues for peace from a victor ... and
we must recognise the dangers inherent in ignoring the wishes
of the powers.*[11]

Saionji annoyed the powerful business lobby by national-
ising the Japanese railways, despite protests from the Mitsubishi combine, which operated many tracks in the southern
island of Kyūshū, and Mitsui, which enjoyed similar controls
in the Osaka area. Saionji's decision led to the resignation of
one of his own cabinet, the Foreign Minister Katō Takaaki,
who was the son-in-law of the president of Mitsubishi.

Traditionally, in the hazy world of court etiquette, a minister's resignation would be expressed in euphemistic terms,
with an outgoing official requesting permission for the return
of his 'skeleton', on account of a conveniently invented
illness. Instead, Saionji broke protocol by telling the Emperor
precisely why Katō was resigning, not because he wished to
damage Katō's standing, but because his position was worthy
of respect, and it was silly to pretend otherwise.[12]

Saionji also aggravated his predecessor Katsura, who had
mistakenly hoped that Saionji would tie up a few loose ends
for him. The 113th Bank of Osaka, in which several of Katsura's cronies owned shares, had been almost ruined by the
Russo-Japanese War, and had only been shored-up by a treas-
ury loan at a preferential rate. Katsura had promised a prominent official a peerage in return for the favour, but met with
short shrift when he asked the new Prime Minister Saionji
to deliver on the promise. Saionji replied that if Katsura had
really valued the man's assistance all that much, he should
have rewarded him for his shady deals when he was in power,
and not asked his successor to do his dirty work.[13]

Saionji's period in office also saw important developments
in what many believed at the time to be merely a minor issue

SOCIALISM UNDER SAIONJI

Saionji's first term saw a relaxation of police suppression of socialism within Japan. Saionji announced to the press that socialism was a global trend that would be tolerated, to some extent, in a Japan under his stewardship. Only a few months later, the Japan Socialist Party obliged by coming out of hiding (where it had been since shortly after its founding in 1906) and entering public life. 'Socialists in those days,' commented Saionji's biographer Takekoshi Yosaburō in 1933, 'were more sensible than they are now.' [14]

The JSP's numbers increased to 2,000 in its first year, after which the party voted at its first annual conference to delete the phrase 'within the limits of the law' from its manifesto. Saionji had, perhaps inadvertently, opened the door to future strikes, protests and conspiracies, although it is unclear whether he knew this all along, and saw such irritations as a necessary part of the development of a healthy democracy. After a JSP-sponsored newspaper in San Francisco publicly insulted the Emperor, Saionji was obliged to backtrack, and banned the JSP once more. [15]

in international diplomacy – Japanese emigration to the United States of America. Japanese emigrants now formed 1 per cent of the population of California. Encouraged to move there under earlier agreements, they had inherited much of the racism aimed at Chinese labourers during the Gold Rush. American sentiments were fanned by a growing literature that depicted Japan as a 'Yellow Peril' – the name had originally been introduced as a racist epithet against the Chinese, but soon encompassed all Asians.

Matters reached a head in 1906, in the aftermath of the San Francisco Earthquake, when a local Board of Education ruled that Japanese children should make up the numbers at an under-attended school for Chinese. It was segregation by another name, and with a career dedicated to attaining equal footing for Japanese in the international community, Saionji was not about to lose ground in America.

News reports of Japanese activities in East Asia, particularly her victory against Russia, a 'European' power, had a mixed effect on Japan's reputation. Ironically, Japan's success against Russia had intensified paranoia about the growing strength of the 'Yellow Peril' and the threat of a war between Japan and another European power. The British author H G Wells, who had found fame by describing a Martian invasion in *The War of the Worlds* (1898), chose a new villainous enemy in his latest work, *The War in the Air* (1907), in which Japan joins forces with China and attacks the United States. In such a climate, Saionji struggled to get an agreement on the emigration issue, but found a compromise by offering the Americans something they wanted in return.

The 'Gentleman's Agreement' of 1907–8 was not a treaty as such, but a series of six communiqués between Saionji's government and that of the US President Theodore Roosevelt. It was agreed that Japan would cease to issue passports to unskilled labourers, but that America would permit Japanese immigrants already in the US to live there with their wives and families. Japanese children would not be segregated in schools. There were holes in the agreement that were disadvantageous to both sides. The Japanese were still subject to discrimination and abuse, with one senator even running for office on a 'Keep California White' campaign. Conversely, the controls did not apply to the Territory of Hawaii, to which Japanese could migrate, before moving on to the mainland with relative ease. The new legislation also had a fatal loophole, in that in allowing Japanese residents to be joined by their families, it encouraged a rise in 'Picture Brides' – arranged marriages *in absentia* between a migrant labourer and a woman from Japan, who would then go to join the 'husband' she had never previously met, who had only ever seen her photograph.

Although of apparently minor significance when set next to Japan's policies in East Asia, the immigration question would prove to be one of the defining issues of Saionji's entire political career. It would ultimately give birth to the 'racial equality' issue, and that would prove to be a crucial topic at the Paris Peace Conference a decade later.

But the aftermath of the Russo-Japanese War continued to cast a shadow over Saionji's administration, and would eventually bring it down. As with his Foreign Ministry following the Sino-Japanese War some years earlier, Saionji attained a position of power in 1906 just in time to clear up someone else's mess. Even as protests continued about the alleged injustice of the Treaty of Portsmouth, Saionji faced complaints from foreign ambassadors in Tokyo, with whose misgivings he would have privately agreed. The British and Americans, who had bankrolled Japan's war effort on the understanding that Manchuria would remain open to their business interests, were the loudest plaintiffs. Chief among their concerns was the behaviour of the Japanese army in Manchuria, where it was slow to withdraw and swift to block the activities of non-Japanese business interests. 'China will find herself,' warned the American Minister, 'at the end of Japanese occupation, the merely nominal sovereign of a territory the material advantages of which have been appropriated by the temporary occupants.' [16]

The issue was a constitutional impasse, with the army claiming that it was obliged to secure the Manchurian frontier, and that the Foreign Ministry had no jurisdiction while martial law was still in force. Saionji attempted to make an informal trip to Manchuria to see for himself, only to have his visit exposed in a hostile Japanese newspaper as an attempt to interfere in a military matter outside his purview. By 1908, the military faction in Tokyo was demanding serious increases in troop levies and military expenditure, to wartime levels even though Japan was now supposedly at peace. Coupled with rising domestic rice prices, the demands were tantamount to imposing wartime conditions on a peacetime government. Saionji was unable to arrange a budget without Katsura's support, and unwilling to carry out such belligerent measures, and consequently resigned in a surprise move on 4 July 1908. Katsura Tarō replaced Saionji as Prime Minister, and served in that role for three years.

8
The Taishō Crisis

The stand-off between Saionji's faction and Katsura's would steer Japanese politics for the following decade. Saionji remained supportive of parliamentary politics; Katsura continued to regard political parties as an irritation that obstructed government by the aristocracy. The Diet was often so delicately balanced that one side was often unable to act without the other, leading the two men to alternate the office of Prime Minister. When Katsura's government fell in 1911, Saionji became Prime Minister once again.

Katsura had not learned his lesson. Even as Saionji took office, Katsura strongly implied that the Emperor had suggested he appoint a particular official as his Foreign Minister. Blunt as ever, Saionji asked him if it really was the Emperor's will, forcing Katsura to admit that it was not.[1]

Saionji's return to power saw him presiding over the confused question of a revolution in China. Representatives of 'Henry' Puyi, the deposed 'Last Emperor' had requested military aid from Japan in suppressing rebels. With the Qing dynasty officially overthrown, Saionji was instead encouraged to throw his support behind the northern warlord Yuan

Shikai, who supposedly entertained plans for a constitutional monarchy. But the collapse of China presented new opportunities for military factions. With China facing the very real prospect of breaking into two southern republics and a Manchu-dominated north, Japanese army officers in Manchuria began efforts to sponsor a Japanese protectorate in Manchuria and Inner Mongolia, and only followed orders to desist with great reluctance. Eventually, Saionji caved in to business interests and offered support to Sun Yatsen, although Sun's failure to gain overall control rendered Japan's offer of arms in return for future trade concessions all but useless.

There were more pressing imperial concerns close to home. Soon after Saionji accepted office, the chief court physician presented him with a secret report that the Meiji Emperor's health was fading fast. In June 1912, the Emperor died, leaving the throne to his heir, the 33-year-old Taishō Emperor. The new ruler, however, had been plagued by ill health throughout his life. As Prime Minister, Saionji was tasked with answering the new ruler's first address, and could not resist sliding a reference to the wider world into the standard platitudes: *Your Majesty will graciously endeavour to enhance to all eternity the glory of the ancestors. This indeed is what the whole world expects and the subject people rely on.*[2]

Saionji's administration, however, did not survive the year, brought down once again by an argument over the armed forces. Saionji refused to approve the army's demand for two new infantry divisions, which led to the resignation of his Minister of War. This now left Saionji vulnerable to the clause introduced by Yamagata some years earlier, which stated that military ministers had to be military men. In protest at Saionji's stance, no serving army officer would agree to fill the vacant post – an act which, Saionji rightly feared, would set a precedent giving the armed forces effective power of veto over any future cabinet decisions.

Saionji resigned, but Katsura Tarō fared no better in replacing him. Instead, Katsura found himself facing additional opposition from the navy, which wanted two new battleships, and refused to appoint a new naval minister until he agreed to it. Frustrated by this, Katsura arranged for an edict from the new Emperor, ordering the navy to appoint a replacement.

Saionji was worried about the constitutional implications of using an imperial order – it would work fine, until the day an errant ministry refused to obey the Emperor's direct command, at which time the nation could be plunged back into civil war. Saionji protested by forming a Movement to Protect Constitutional Government with allies in the Diet. Others, however, were not so peaceful, and the Katsura administration was brought down by mass demonstrations and riots in Tokyo. Saionji did not attempt to replace Katsura. Instead, he resigned from his own party and went into retirement. The post of Japanese Prime Minister passed, ominously, into the hands of an admiral, and then to the retired statesman Ōkuma Shigenobu.

However, even as he officially left party politics behind, Saionji was recalled to a new role, when the young Taishō Emperor asked if he would 'assist' him. This innocent-seeming request amounted to Saionji's appointment as what would be the last of the *genrō* – a group of elders whose advice to the Emperor often carried an indirect force that could contend with decisions in the Diet. Although the formal powers of the *genrō* were limited, they were able to steer cabinet appointments to the extent that they could sometimes limit the power of unwelcome ministries.

However, the power of the *genrō* was mortally damaged

by the new precedents for military interference in national policy, and the new administration soon went to war. The precise terms of the Anglo-Japanese Alliance did not require Japan to enter the First World War on the British side, but Prime Minister Ōkuma decided to do so anyway, as a means of seizing German possessions in the Pacific, and of consolidating Japan's position in China.

In his ultimatum to Germany, Ōkuma made a great point of citing Japan's obligations under the Anglo-Japanese Alliance. In supposed deference to Japan's deal with Britain, Ōkuma proposed to '… take measures to remove the causes of all disturbance of peace in the Far East, and to safeguard general interests … to secure firm and enduring peace in Eastern Asia … '. Ironically, such a claim was made against the faint protests of the British Foreign Secretary, Arthur Balfour, who cautioned against any acts by the Japanese that might lead to 'unfounded misapprehension' about Japan's intentions in Asia.[3]

The problem, as the British saw it, was that Japan would be seen to be embarking upon a feverish land-grab under the cover of assisting its European ally. However, the Japanese Foreign Minister Makino Nobuaki saw it very differently. He noted that Japan had poured vast amounts of investment into certain Chinese regions. The money might be 'industrial' rather than 'political', but Makino pointed out that for industrial investments to be secure, China required a secure government. For China to have secure government, the Japanese might be expected to interfere in Chinese matters, be it through shoring-up unstable regimes or offering support to particular politicians or political parties.

Makino's rhetoric reflected a common conception among Tokyo politicians in 1914, that Japan and China required *teikei* (literally 'accord') on a vast range of policies. The two countries, it was believed, needed to establish trade deals, commercial liaisons, railway projects, and even political agreements with each other, in order to present a united front towards, and perhaps even against, the white races.

To some extent, Chinese policymakers had even agreed with the theory behind the Japanese plan. In August 1914, Yuan Shikai had reportedly said that: 'China, like Japan is of the yellow race, and should not all make friends of the Europeans and Americans who are of the white race?' But he had added that, once the First World War was over, China and Japan might expect 'more powerful white adversaries', against whom they might need to cooperate.[4]

Such talk is one of the earliest incidences of a policy that would come to dominate Japanese militarism in the first half of the 20th century – the idea that Japan should become the hegemon of a 'Great East Asian Co-Prosperity Sphere', forming a bloc of nations that could stand up to the European powers. It was naturally assumed that China would be too weak to lead itself.

But even if Yuan Shikai had offered vague and positive approval towards general Japanese statements of intent, he does not seem to have wanted them to put such theories into practice. Despite his protestations, the Japanese launched their attack on German possessions in the Pacific, capturing a number of small islands and, most notoriously, invading Chinese territory in order to oust the Germans from Shandong.

Japanese forces attacked the German naval base on the Shandong Peninsula in December 1914, shortly after war was officially declared. The 23,000 Japanese troops were accompanied by a small force of 1,500 British soldiers. The port town of Qingdao (Tsingtao) held out for two months, but eventually surrendered – neutralising an important German military site, but also effectively leaving a piece of Chinese territory in Japanese hands. Out in the Pacific, the Japanese navy took the initiative, seizing the Marianas, the Carolines and the Marshall Islands without resistance. If the navy exceeded Tokyo's orders by doing so, there were no complaints.

The physical attacks were followed with a diplomatic one in January 1915, with the presentation to China of the Twenty-One Demands, which might be broadly summarised in five groups as:

1. The Japanese acquisition of Shandong was confirmed (i.e. left to Japan, the *de facto* occupier, and Germany, the soon-to-be-vanquished former occupier, to determine).
2. Japan was to gain further rights of settlement and occupation along the South Manchuria Railway, effectively extending Japanese influence into Manchuria itself.
3. Several Chinese mines and refineries with Japanese shareholders were to be handed over to full Japanese control.
4. China was to offer no further territorial concessions to foreign powers, except Japan.
5. A cluster of further deals establishing Japanese control of the Chinese police force, Chinese arms trade, Chinese government offices, and the vague yet intimidating right of Japanese missionaries to 'preach' in China.

Saionji's biographers are strangely silent on the matter of the Twenty-One Demands. Saionji had resigned from both government and party, but as a *genrō* he would have presumably seen the Twenty-One Demands before they were presented to Yuan Shikai. Saionji's position on China, throughout the preceding years of his career, had been that Japan and China might bring mutual benefit to one another through Japanese investments and industry. Perhaps that was the reasoning behind Makino's rhetoric on the lack of any essential difference between political and industrial obligations – Saionji might have favoured peaceful invest-ment, but the Ōkuma cabinet now believed that peace was threatened, and with it the investments already in place in China.

There was also a belief among some Japanese politicians, widespread enough to bear repeating here, that the Twenty-One Demands were a favour to China. Amid the frantic argu-ments that broke out in Beijing, one Japanese envoy offered the bizarre defence that 'demanding' such concessions from China was simply a matter of protocol:

'I want to tell you that Japan put in the demands to help China … . Japan thinks the Asiatics should be amalgamated into one co-operative whole to combat the white race. The first blow in this direction will be made through China. China cannot, after all, offer to give Japan what we want. The demands are to make it easier – to give [China] the excuse of bending to force … What we suggest is good strategy. It is plain you need someone to run your country. We propose to do that for you. If Britain and America thought that China was inviting us to be its guide, they would apply pressure to prevent you. But when Japan demands – ah, that is a different matter. They can screech their heads off, and Japan will not give a fig for what they say.'[5]

However, since the Twenty-One Demands were initially presented in secret, and the Japanese would attempt to keep the Chinese from revealing them to the outside world, it is unclear how this would present much of a defence.

Although the Chinese unwillingly agreed to the first four groups of Demands, the nature of negotiations would become an important issue at the Paris Peace Conference that followed the war. China would eventually enter the war as an Ally – in other words, on the 'same side' as Japan. Chinese diplomats would later argue that this made Japanese pressure an unseemly and invalid act against a fellow enemy of Germany.

Japan's role in the First World War was initially restricted to the Pacific theatre. In February 1915, Japanese marines formed part of a police action against a mutiny in Singapore by Indian soldiers. In late 1916, four Japanese warships were sent on a long journey to the Mediterranean after a British request for naval aid in the European theatre. Based in Malta, the ships sailed on several hundred escort missions in the Mediterranean, and also took part in the rescue of over 7,000 seamen. In return, it was quietly agreed that Britain would support Japan's desire to hold on to Shandong after the war was over.

This agreement was to sow much discord at the Paris Peace Conference, particularly in the wake of America's entry into the war in 1917. America did not share Britain's willingness to turn a blind eye to Japanese expansion into Shandong, and the position of America and Japan as new allies was placed under threat by increasing tensions over Japan's actions in the Pacific. In an attempt to calm things down, the US Secretary of State Robert Lansing and the Japanese envoy Ishii Kikujirō concluded the Lansing-Ishii Agreement in 1917. This shaky compromise restated an old 'Open Door' policy, in which both America and Japan agreed to uphold Chinese territorial integrity. The US, however, also acknowledged that Japan had 'special interests' in China.

A cynic might have argued that the Lansing-Ishii Agreement amounted to nothing, since 'special interests' might be taken to override any of the previous good intentions over Chinese territorial integrity. A secret rider to the agreement asserted that neither power would attempt to take advantage of the war in pursuing territorial gains at the expense of other allies. Although this might seem to have amounted to an agreement to leave Shandong, the Japanese could (and indeed would) argue later in Paris that:

a) Shandong was a possession of Germany, not an Ally.
b) Although China was an Ally, Shandong had belonged to Germany before the war, and belonged to Japan at the time that the Lansing-Ishii Agreement was made.

The Lansing-Ishii Agreement may have eased tensions between Japan and the US, but would prove to be of little use in protecting Chinese interests after the war. Meanwhile, Japan continued to expand into China, with the conclusion of the Nishihara Loans, a series of eight huge cash injections, given to China on the understanding that Japan could keep Shandong after the war, along with a number of other concessions that were tantamount to the reintroduction of the fifth group of the Twenty-One Demands. The deal was made with the Chinese leader Duan Qirui – who was attacked for his decision after the conditions were leaked, and who his successors would claim was not empowered to make such guarantees on China's behalf.

The outbreak of revolution and civil war in Russia would open up a new front for the Japanese. US President Woodrow

Wilson requested 7,000 Japanese soldiers to help in an international relief effort for a 'Siberian Intervention' – a deployment of troops in aid of anti-Bolshevik forces in eastern Russia. Japan agreed but sent ten times the agreed number, and not as part of the coalition but under direct Japanese command.

Shortly after the commencement of the Siberian Intervention in November 1918, the First World War came to an end, with thousands of Japanese troops on Chinese and Russian soil, and with the Japanese navy occupying several strategically-important Pacific islands that had once belonged to Germany. The incumbent administration in Tokyo hoped to consolidate these gains and keep them in peacetime, which would require some deft negotiation at the forthcoming Paris Peace Conference.

The Siberian Intervention was intended by Japanese militarists as the first phase of the creation of a puppet state in Siberia. Initial plans to advance as far as Lake Baikal were curbed after American protests. The immense over-deployment by the Japanese army was regarded with deep suspicion by other powers, and would damage Japanese diplomacy for several years, until the troops were removed in 1922. In nominally supporting 'White' Russians against the Bolshevik 'Reds' who eventually won the Russian Civil War, Japan would also experience early difficulties in diplomatic relations which what would become the Soviet Union.

Remembering the fate of Katsura Tarō after the Russo-Japanese War and the embarrassment of the Treaty of Portsmouth, it was also deemed important to send a delegation headed by a man who could be seen to transcend party politics. Japan needed a representative of extraordinary stature, preferably someone who would be regarded by the other powers as an internationalist and diplomat, and not a warmonger like the administration that he would have to represent. Japan needed Saionji Kinmochi.

Prince Saionji in a portrait by Sir William Orpen, painted in Paris during the peace treaty conferences. Saionji was born into the highest rank of Japanese hereditary nobility and was elevated from marquis to prince in 1920.

Orpen commented: 'The marquis sat, never for one second did his expression give an inkling of what his brain was thinking about. He never moved: his eyelids never fluttered.'

II

The Paris Peace Conference

9

The Faults of the Past

Tokyo initially underestimated the importance of the Paris Peace Conference, and intended to send a delegation led by someone of ambassadorial rank. It was only when Chinda Sutemi, the Japanese ambassador to Great Britain, cabled a report on the other delegations that the error became apparent. The Great Powers were all sending their Prime Ministers or Presidents, but the choice was not quite so simple for the Japanese. For European delegates, Paris was only a few days away. For the Japanese, it would be a trip of several weeks. Moreover, the *Seiyūkai* majority in the Diet was feeble at best – the new Prime Minister Hara Kei could not well afford to leave Japan with so many pressing domestic issues. With every other nation sending what Chinda called 'statesmen of the first rank', Japan was obliged to provide someone similar or risk a diplomatic gaffe.

Saionji's selection was based in part on his strong connections with Europe, but largely on domestic considerations. Hara and Yamagata, who were the prime decision-makers behind Saionji's appointment, wanted a popular figure at the Conference in order to enjoy cross-party support for whatever decisions that Conference might hand down – there were fears all round that otherwise the incumbent administration would take the credit, or the blame. Ironically, although it was understood in Japan that Saionji, a *genrō* and a nobleman, was a far more prestigious delegate than a mere Prime Minister, the traditional Japanese respect for 'retired' potentates was almost entirely lost on the Peace Conference delegates, some of whom assumed they were being fobbed off with a figurehead.[1]

The choice of Saionji to head the delegation surprised many observers, including the British Ambassador, who had expected the post would go to Baron Katō Takaaki (1860–1926). Katō had served as the Japanese ambassador to Britain and had been a Foreign Minister in four cabinets, including those of Itō Hirobumi and Saionji himself (from which he had acrimoniously resigned over railway nationalisation). Katō had strong links to the Mitsubishi industrial combine, and was a regular opponent of the *genrā* Saionji's biographers claim that Katō was never an option – some other sources claim that the *threat* that the post might go to Katō was a factor that encouraged Saionji to take the position himself.

Saionji insisted upon the selection of Makino Nobuaki (1861–1949) as his right-hand man. The two men had known each other since at least the Iwakura Mission of 1871, when Makino had been a boy of only 10. He had served at Japan's London embassy, as a prefectural governor in Japan, and also as Ambassador to Austria and Italy, before becoming the Education Minister in Saionji's first cabinet. He was very much a creation of Itō Hirobumi and Saionji, and shared their political position.

The third high-ranking member of the delegation was Viscount Chinda Sutemi (1857–1929), another diplomat with a good track-record in foreign relations. In the late 1870s, he had studied for four years at an American university, before returning home to take up a post with the Foreign Ministry. He served on diplomatic missions to Britain, Korea, China and the Netherlands, and was on the commission that supervised the peace treaty that ended the Russo-Japanese War. Chinda was also a Christian, a rare and exotic creature in Japan, but likely to give him some common ground with some of the European delegates. Some 60 other delegates included the Japanese ambassador in Paris, Matsui Keishiro, a Lieutenant-General, a Vice-Admiral, a Doctor of Laws and several businessmen, as well as secretaries and Saionji's daughter and son-in-law.

Even as Saionji agreed to the mission, there were suggestions that Japan could not afford to lose him at such a critical time. Shortly after Saionji's ship left for Europe, the venerable Yamagata Aritomo fell seriously ill, and officials hatched a contingency plan to recall him if matters worsened.

Anecdotes about the journey of the Japanese delegation show Saionji gruffly hounding the younger delegates, and often failing to impress upon them the need for diplomats to behave diplomatically. In particular, he was troubled by the attitude of the young Konoe Fumimaro (1891–1945), a princely prodigy, whose grandfather had taught Saionji calligraphy, and whose father had once been Saionji's secretary in Austria-Hungary. Like Saionji, Konoe was an heir to one of the most powerful branches of the Fujiwara clan, and might be said, at least in terms of protocol, to outrank Saionji himself. In 1914 he had published his own translation of Oscar Wilde's *The Soul of Man Under Socialism* in a magazine, leading to the banning of the issue in which it appeared. He also took a passionate interest in a newspaper for which he was a major shareholder – in his attitude and demeanour, he greatly resembled the dandyish young Saionji, although the old Saionji would not have enjoyed the comparison. On political matters, the two were often diametrically opposed.

The first sign of trouble between the men came in Ceylon, when the Japanese party put ashore at Colombo, and Konoe and his cronies picked flowers in a local park. An angry Saionji was heard berating the diplomats like naughty children: *How can you be so ill-mannered? Behave yourselves, or I shall never take you abroad again!*

Saionji became similarly irate as the ship neared Marseilles, when he overheard Konoe's gang discussing the best means of getting past customs inspectors without attracting undue attention. *With such an attitude*, Saionji fumed, *how can you pretend to be respectable gentlemen, dignitaries on the international stage?*

Konoe's misbehaviour would continue in Paris, and came to a head when, as a mere aide, he was excluded from one of the Conference meetings. Instead, he gained access by posing as a journalist from the Japanese newspaper in which he was a shareholder.

If you continue to behave like this, Saionji said, *I will have to dismiss you from the delegation.*[2]

However, the worst of Konoe's indiscretions had been committed before the Japanese delegates even left home. On 15 December 1918, Konoe wrote an article for the journal *Nihon oyobi Nihonjin* (*Japan and the Japanese*), which was sharply critical of what he saw as the Anglo-American bias of the Conference: 'Japanese opinion leaders are so enthralled by the spectacular pronouncements of Anglo-American politicians that they cannot perceive the conscious and unconscious ways in which the democracy and humanitarianism put forward by Anglo-American spokesmen provide a mask for their own self-interest.'[3]

Konoe was forceful and rhetorically repetitive; he returned again and again to the idea of Paris as a cloak for the self-interest of the white race. Although he conceded that some of the negative influences of the Conference might be both 'conscious and unconscious', Konoe boldly stated some unwelcome truths, not only about the way that the Conference might be regarded in the non-white world, but also about the form that Japan's reaction, in its own self-interest, might take.

'In the coming Peace Conference, should we decide to join the League of Nations, we must demand ... the eradication of economic imperialism and discriminatory treatment of Asian peoples by Caucasians. Militarism is not the only force that violates justice and humanity. Economic imperialism, also, by enabling the most powerful to monopolize enormous amounts of capital and natural resources, prevents the free development of other nations and enriches the imperialists without requiring the use of force. Should the Peace Conference fail to suppress this rampant economic imperialism, the Anglo-American powers will become the masters of the

> Should the Peace Conference fail to suppress ... rampant economic imperialism, the Anglo-American powers will become the masters of the world.
>
> KONOE FUMIMARO

world and, in the name of preserving the status quo, dominate it through the League of Nations and arms reduction, thus serving their own selfish interests ... Should their policy prevail, Japan, which is small, resource-poor, and unable to consume all its own industrial products, would have no resort but to destroy the status quo for the sake of self-preservation, just like Germany.'[4]

The ripples from the article, with the uncompromising title of 'Reject the Anglo-American-centred Peace' would follow the delegation along its journey, causing adverse reactions in Chinese translation and in Europe itself. Saionji knew of Konoe's article, but clearly had not expected it to find a readership outside Japan, where it may have revealed some of the delegation's plans. Konoe's words were all the more unwelcome because he had, inadvertently or otherwise, revealed the secret position of the Japanese government. Tokyo was apprehensive about the League. Although internationalists like Saionji were broadly in agreement with its aims, the Japanese government was concerned about their implication for their access to natural resources, particularly fuel, raw materials and *lebensraum*. Saionji and the other delegates had been instructed to delay the League for as long as possible, and if that aim failed, to ensure that a clause for racial equality was inserted into its covenant.[5] Although the Americans did not know the precise nature of Saionji's instructions, their diplomatic intelligence had already noted the mood of the times to which Konoe's article was playing. Wilson's ambassador in Tokyo, George Morris, had reported in November 1918: 'It is hoped by the Japanese that the organization of a League of Nations will offer an opportunity to assert the equality of the yellow race, a question which underlies all discussions on the subject.'[6]

Plainly, Saionji thought that it would be impossible to delay the League, and was probably fully intending to ignore the first part of his order – giving up on it as a lost cause and pressing instead for racial equality. Nor were his intentions likely to have been unknown to Tokyo, since his protégé Makino had refused to go to Paris unless the Japanese government promised to back him on the idea of joining and supporting the League. Regardless, with Saionji maintaining his customary silence, Konoe's article gained extra authority, and made it sound as if the Japanese were hoping to delay or avoid entirely the creation of a League of Nations.

Upon his arrival in France, Saionji did what he could to control the damage, issuing a statement that appeared on the surface to be a rebuttal of Konoe's article, but actually merely rephrased it in a more diplomatic fashion. He told *Le Petit Marseillais*: *I have no hesitation in telling you that Japan desires to organize a League of Nations as soon as possible, in order to ensure a civilisation for the entire world that is 'freer, more effective and above all fruitful in results.' In this century of vertiginous progress in which we live, it is necessary for men of all classes and all races to lend their co-operation in the destruction of all those elements – such as Prussian militarism – which are likely to stop or even delay the progress of civilization.*[7]

But Konoe, for all his imprudence, had also hit at least one nail squarely on the head. Although his version of the situation was far more discreet, Saionji was still obliged to concede: *The peace that issues from this Conference cannot be solely a European peace, but moreover a peace for the entire world, and assured forever. Humanity must acknowledge the faults of the past, if she is able to live happily in a peace that is eternal and fruitful.*[8]

The prognosis was not good – having checked in at their headquarters at the Hotel Bristol, the Japanese had to look hard to find their issues anywhere on the agenda. Woodrow Wilson's Fourteen Points, outlining his blueprint for a lasting peace, were European-focused and did not mention Japan or China at all, concentrating instead on what were, to the Japanese, trivial issues such as Alsace-Lorraine and Montenegro. Tokyo had plainly been expecting that the Japanese, as allies of the victors, would enjoy pride of place among the Great Powers. Instead, they were only permitted two delegates at the meetings of the Council of Ten, and in the rare full meetings

PRESIDENT WILSON'S FOURTEEN POINTS, 8 JANUARY 1918

The program of the world's peace, therefore, is our program; and that program, the only possible program, as we see it, is this:

I. Open covenants of peace, openly arrived at, after which there shall be no private international understandings of any kind but diplomacy shall proceed always frankly and in the public view.

II. Absolute freedom of navigation upon the seas, outside territorial waters, alike in peace and in war, except as the seas may be closed in whole or in part by international action for the enforcement of international covenants.

III. The removal, so far as possible, of all economic barriers and the establishment of an equality of trade conditions among all the nations consenting to the peace and associating themselves for its maintenance.

IV. Adequate guarantees given and taken that national armaments will be reduced to the lowest point consistent with domestic safety.

V. A free, open-minded, and absolutely impartial adjustment of all colonial claims, based upon a strict observance of the principle that in determining all such questions of sovereignty the interests of the populations concerned must have equal weight with the equitable claims of the government whose title is to be determined.

VI. The evacuation of all Russian territory and such a settlement of all questions affecting Russia as will secure the best and freest cooperation of the other nations of the world in obtaining for her an unhampered and unembarrassed opportunity for the independent determination of her own political development and national policy and assure her of a sincere welcome into the society of free nations under institutions of her own choosing; and, more than a welcome, assistance also of every kind that she may need and may herself desire. The treatment accorded Russia by her sister nations in the months to come will be the acid test of their good will, of their comprehension of her needs as distinguished from their own interests, and of their intelligent and unselfish sympathy.

VII. Belgium, the whole world will agree, must be evacuated and restored, without any attempt to limit the sovereignty which she enjoys in common with all other free nations. No other single act will serve as this will serve to restore confidence among the nations in the laws which they have themselves set and determined for the government of their relations with one another. Without this healing act the whole structure and validity of international law is forever impaired.

VIII. All French territory should be freed and the invaded portions restored, and the wrong done to France by Prussia in 1871 in the matter of Alsace-Lorraine, which has unsettled the peace of the world for nearly fifty years, should be righted, in order that peace may once more be made secure in the interest of all.

IX. A readjustment of the frontiers of Italy should be effected along clearly recognizable lines of nationality.

X. The peoples of Austria-Hungary, whose place among the nations we wish to see safeguarded and assured, should be accorded the freest opportunity to autonomous development.

XI. Rumania, Serbia, and Montenegro should be evacuated; occupied territories restored; Serbia accorded free and secure access to the sea; and the relations of the several Balkan states to one another determined by friendly counsel along historically established lines of allegiance and nationality; and international guarantees of the political and economic independence and territorial integrity of the several Balkan states should be entered into.

XII. The Turkish portion of the present Ottoman Empire should be assured a secure sovereignty, but the other nationalities which are now under Turkish rule should be assured an undoubted security of life and an absolutely unmolested opportunity of autonomous development, and the Dardanelles should be permanently opened as a free passage to the ships and commerce of all nations under international guarantees.

XIII. An independent Polish state should be erected which should include the territories inhabited by indisputably Polish populations, which should be assured a free and secure access to the sea, and whose political and economic independence and territorial integrity should be guaranteed by international covenant.

XIV. A general association of nations must be formed under specific covenants for the purpose of affording mutual guarantees of political independence and territorial integrity to great and small states alike.

of the full Peace Conference, they were sat far down the end of the long tables, facing the delegations from Ecuador, Guatemala and the Middle East. Saionji's own chair, should he ever take it, was across the table from that of Emir Feisal.

The Japanese were also kept out of the meetings of the inner council, a decision that was justified by Wilson on the feeble pretext that although Saionji and Makino had been Prime Ministers in the past, neither of them was currently serving in that capacity, whereas the other attendees – Wilson, Clemenceau, Lloyd George and Orlando – were incumbents. This was, as everyone could see, very shaky ground, and Wilson's foreign policy adviser Colonel House assured Makino that the Japanese would have the power to approve the decisions made in their absence. Consequently, the central decision-makers are remembered as the Big Four, and not the 'Big Five' as the Japanese would have surely preferred.

> Amiable Prince Saionji, impetuous once, today quietly ironical, an old comrade of mine at the lectures of our law professor, Émile Acollas.
> GEORGES CLEMENCEAU

In later life, Georges Clemenceau would feign fond memories of the Japanese delegation, remembering ' ... Baron Matsui, a massive chunk of Japanese mentality, who spoke little, but did not shrink from speaking out. Amiable Prince Saionji, impetuous once, today quietly ironical, an old comrade of mine at the lectures of our law professor Émile Acollas. Count Makino, understanding and reserved.' But others recall a very different Clemenceau, loudly asking 'what the little man had said' when Makino spoke, and once archly observing the bitter irony of being trapped in a room with the 'ugly' Japanese, when there was a city of blonde women just outside the door.[9]

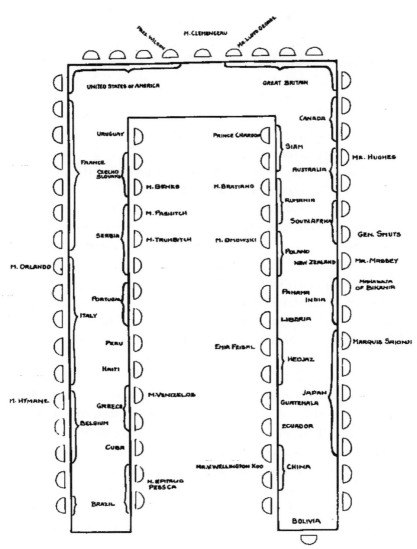

Sketch of the seating plan at the Paris Peace Conference.

Despite occasional press speculation as to Saionji's whereabouts, he was a visible presence at many important meetings. He sat in on all the meetings of the Preliminary Peace Conference, and also on all but one of the Council of Ten sessions in March. However, he made no comments. When Saionji was absent, his underlings often let him down, at least in the eyes of the Great Powers. Chinda spoke English well enough, Makino less so, but other Japanese delegates were sometimes found to be lacking in the necessary linguistic ability to follow the debates. One committee member, when asked if he voted 'aye or nay', answered with an inscrutable 'Yes'.[10]

Behind the scenes, even those who admired Saionji remained suspicious of Japanese aims in Paris, and many continued to resent the way in which Japan's nominal status as an Ally had swept many such 'faults of the past' under the carpet. Stephen Bonsal, who had seen Japanese foreign policy at work first-hand in 1895 with the murder of Queen Min in Korea, was uncompromising in his opinions: 'Japan, the great law- and treaty-breaker in the Far East, sits in the Council of the Great Powers and is not even to be interrogated as to her recent conduct.'[11]

Saionji's luck was not all bad. His links with France made him the darling of the French newspapers, leading one to comment: 'It is not possible for there to have been a better choice than this man.'[12] Occasional salacious speculations in the local press about Saionji's love life should, perhaps, be regarded in a more Gallic manner – in admiring his mistress, the French may have been expressing a form of sly esteem, rather than the censure that has been perceived by some Anglo-American historians.

Saionji had an additional lucky break with the Korean question, which Japan's status as an official Ally had essentially removed from the table. This was not known at the time by the Koreans themselves, who had heard of Wilson's Fourteen Points with mounting excitement, and homed in on the notion of 'self-determination'. The first protests were heard in Japan itself, where Korean students hosted the reading of a Korean 'Declaration of Independence'.

In Korea itself, Gojong, the widower of the ill-fated Queen Min, died in January 1919, spurring political groups in Korea to stage an uprising ahead of his funeral. Understanding the Peace Conference to be a super-national agency of justice, the Korean independence movement hoped to send delegates to Paris to plead the country's case against Japan. The Japanese colonial powers in Korea did their utmost to nip such talk in the bud, refusing exit visas to putative delegates.

A protest in Seoul on 1 March saw the same declaration read aloud, but as demonstrations spread, the Japanese initiated a clampdown. In the atrocities that followed, Japanese troops were said to have machine-gunned protesters at one rally, while Japanese police were alleged to have trapped protestors in another town inside a burning church. In all, some 7,000 Koreans are said to have died in what is known as the March 1st Movement. They died without knowing that the Paris Peace Conference had already given up on their cause two weeks earlier, when the entreaties of a Korean émigré and his American associate had failed to interest the Great Powers in Korea's plight.

With no visas issued from Korea itself, the Korean case was in the hands of those expatriates who were already outside the Japanese sphere of influence. Almost three million Korean refugees had fled their homeland for China and Russia, and hoped that the Peace Conference would put an end to Japanese domination on the peninsula. The Koreans in China had sent one General Pak, so impoverished by his change in circumstances that he was obliged to walk along the tracks of the Trans-Siberian Railway. He did not make it to the Peace Conference in time, which left the pleading of the Korean case in the hands of Kim Kyusik, who had come to speak for the Korean refugees in China, even though he was truly representing Korea's provisional government in exile.[13]

Kim found a sympathetic ear in Stephen Bonsal. The heroic General Pak had been Bonsal's personal interpreter in 1895, and Bonsal's love of Korea and distrust of Japan spurred him to push Kim's case with Colonel House. It was the best chance that the Koreans had of gaining the attention of the Conference, and Bonsal did his utmost to persuade House, and hence Wilson, that the Koreans deserved a voice. Bonsal was swiftly knocked back – Japanese colonial interests in Korea had been formally recognised by American Presidents Roosevelt and Taft, and Wilson was not about to overturn the status quo over what was regarded as a 'local' matter. Bonsal offered his Korean friends a small sop – that the forthcoming League of Nations might be in a better position to police Japanese activities: 'If we deal out justice in Europe and punish the criminals here it may prove a leaven of righteousness in other fields. Perhaps later the League will be able to curb Japan when it has less pressing matters nearer at hand to deal with. I hope so, but it was hard to have to tell Kim that there was not even a forlorn hope that he would have his day in court, that Japan, if not a Great Power, is certainly a strong one.'[14]

Bonsal was left dejected by his failure. 'In some respects,' he wrote, 'I fear the New Order is very like the Old ... Korea is far away ... but in it live some twenty million people who are being oppressed and whose enslavement ... may result in another explosion, another World War.'[15] Before the Paris Peace Conference was over, Korean émigrés took matters into their own hands. The loose association of refugees was transformed into a Provisional Government of the Republic of Korea, which met in Shanghai. This government in exile would continue to press for Korea's cause over the following two decades.

Saionji did what he could to ameliorate the fears of his fellow delegates, and made several gestures to establish the idea that just as the Conference might wish to meddle in Asia, so Japan might contribute meaningfully to European matters. Most surprising to many of his associates was his open support for the Kaiser to be put on trial. It was a statement from a supposed monarchist that shocked several

> In some respects, I fear the New Order is very like the Old.
>
> STEPHEN BONSAL

interested parties, most notably the British King George V, the Kaiser's cousin, to whom Saionji was later obliged to explain himself.[16]

But Saionji's most impressive concession, and a sign of his superb cunning once more at work, was his stance on Russian claims in the Mediterranean. Despite the legacy of the Russo-Japanese War, Saionji claimed that he was ready to fight for a Russian cause if it were in the interests of Europe as a whole:

To Japan, to all our people, I am not speaking merely for myself, the Conference will have failed in one of its high purposes unless the Russians are placed in control of Constantinople and the Dardanelles. They must have a base there that will give them free access to the warm waters of the Mediterranean. I do not say this merely in recognition of our pledges to the Russian people. I have also in mind the interests of

Europe. I am of the opinion that Russia's agricultural produce and her increasing industrial output will revive the devastated economy of Europe as nothing else can ...[17]

However, Colonel House saw through Saionji's scheme within moments, commenting to his aide: 'What a wise old boy he is. Certainly, the outlet on the Mediterranean would keep Russia busy in Europe for decades to come and give Japan for the same period a free hand in Manchuria, in Siberia, and indeed the whole of Asia. What a boon that would be for Japan – and what disaster for China.'[18]

10

An Anglo-American Peace

Ironically, considering their disagreements, Konoe Fumimaro is one of the sole reliable sources for Saionji's daily activities in Paris. Although non-Japanese writers often repeat the idea of Saionji as an idle or absent figure, Konoe's Paris diary paints a very different picture. Saionji spent most mornings in meetings with his own delegation and embassy staff; this was when he also gave press conferences to keep the audience at home informed. He spent most afternoons in the offices of the Japanese delegation, and many evenings reading over reports from the delegates who had attended the Conference proper. Evenings were also the time when he conducted informal meetings with Allied figures. A Japanese historian would be scandalised at the suggestion that Saionji did nothing at the Conference – he worked full-time with his own delegation, but seems to have been damned by posterity for not making conspicuous appearances and statements in the presence of the non-Japanese delegates or press.

Occasional variations in the routine have become the only trips reported in some sources – he did go for a drive on several occasions, usually to show his daughter Shinko and her husband some of the Parisian sights from his own youth. He also frequented a Parisian tailor on several occasions, but otherwise his work for the Japanese delegation was dedicated and somewhat beyond the call of duty for an ailing near-septuagenarian. The international press took greater interest in his 24-year-old companion Ohana, the latest in his string of geisha mistresses. Conspicuously vivacious and attractive at a conference which largely comprised ageing men, Ohana caused something of a stir, particularly when Woodrow Wilson gave her an expensive necklace as a gift.[1]

Events had conspired to take Korea off the table, and Saionji's support of Russian interests in the Mediterranean was of little practical value. His main remaining tasks at Versailles were twofold – the retention of former German possessions in the Far East, and the insertion of a clause into the covenant of the League of Nations that enforced racial equality among members.

Regarding German possessions in the Pacific, the Japanese already enjoyed strong support. In return for Japanese naval assistance in 1917, the British had already recognised their claims, as had Italy, France and Russia. However, it was widely understood, by delegates on all sides, that Japan's activities in the war had solely served its own interests. Even the British, who had agreed to 'support' Japanese claims in the same 1917 agreement, felt mildly aggrieved that their involvement in the war had not been more active. It was felt by many, not merely at the Conference, but also in the press, that the Japanese guarantee of military support had not been quite as useful as the 1917 parties had hoped.[2]

This had already been made abundantly clear to the Japanese in Beijing, where a chargé d'affaires had asked George Morrison, chief adviser to the Chinese delegation, to give his honest opinion on others' view of Japan. Morrison, never one to hold back, let him have it.

'I said there was not an Englishman who knew his facts who did not consider that Japan had failed to fulfil her obligations as an ally and I spoke of the bitterness felt by her failure … We knew that the Japanese military were to a large extent sympathetic with Germany … I told him what was the truth regarding the extraordinary care taken by the British Government to prevent any criticism … from appearing in any English newspaper [despite] the hostilities of the Japanese press.'[3]

'Who can say,' said Clemenceau, 'that in the war [Japan] played a part that can be compared for instance with that of France? Japan defended its interests in the Far East, but when she was requested to intervene in Europe, everyone knows what the answer of Japan was.'[4]

Anti-Japanese feelings also ran high in America, particularly on the west coast, which regarded itself as under threat from Japanese immigration, and in the south, where Japanese interference in the Mexican Civil War was regarded with suspicion. A 1917 suggestion by a German diplomat that Japan and Mexico join forces against the United States was no help either. But Wilson had other issues on his mind – beyond these popular bugbears of the day, he was worried about America's own interests in the Pacific. Arguably, the country's constant westward advancement had not stopped at all in California, but now raged across the Pacific. The Philippines had fallen to the USA in 1898, leading to further acquisitions on Guam and Hawaii, at least in part to provide naval support to that far-flung territory. American and Japanese interests in the Pacific, even if not immediately adjacent, were sure to be soon enough. The prospect, however, remote, that the United States and Japan might be at odds, was sufficient to worry delegates from Canada, sure to be caught in the middle if fighting reached the American Pacific coast. Wilson had an additional concern, which was that the main nexus of trans-Pacific telegraph cables was on the obscure island of Yap, within the Japanese claims. If Japan got what it wanted, its navy would not only have an uncontested series of bases stretching across a thousand miles, from Hokkaidō to Taiwan, down to Palau, but a stranglehold on communications.

Delegates from other states in the British Empire had similar worries. Granting Japan territorial rights over the Marshall Islands, the Marianas and the Carolines brought Japan's sphere of influence perilously close to New Zealand and Australia – in fact, since the Australian demands included the neighbouring Bismarck Archipelago and the former German New Guinea, Japan and Australia would effectively share a common border.

Eventually, a series of compromises saved face at the Conference, and Japan got what it wanted. Robert Cecil and Jan Smuts offered a solution that presented differing levels of mandate, dependent on the territory's perceived ability to manage its own affairs. The attitude of delegates on all sides towards the Pacific islands was one of jocular racism – there were many gags about cannibals, and Billy Hughes even commented that he wanted more missionaries in New Guinea so that the locals would have a better food supply. Consequently, it was little surprise when, keen to move on to more important (i.e. European) matters in the Conference, the delegates accepted the notion that the Pacific Islands were a C-class mandate. This would hand them over to Japanese supervision for a notional lease period of 999 years. In return, the Japanese, like all other states with C-class territories, were expected to keep the islands demilitarised, not to build naval bases or otherwise fortify them, and to observe restrictions on the sale of alcohol and firearms.[5]

Since the League of Nations was the first item of business on the agenda, the racial equality clause was the first real point of contention for the Japanese delegation. On terms of self-interest, the aims of the Japanese were clear – a commitment to racial equality for League members would be a vital, crucial lever in pushing Japanese interests in America. It would, if carried, force the Californian government to permit Japanese immigration, allow such immigrants to own land, bring in their spouses and for their children to attend unsegregated schools. The Japanese, however, were not solely interested in America, or even in immigration. In 1918, Viscount Ishii had observed that there were unfair import restrictions on, for example, Japanese goods in French Indo-China, even at a time when the Japanese Navy was supposedly fighting to protect the region from Germany.[6]

But it was immigration that was the sticking-point for all the white powers with Pacific coastlines. If passed, the proposals would undo a decade of anti-Japanese legislation in America, and destroy the White Australia policy. To these and many other delegates, there was also the terrifying prospect that the inequities of a Most Favoured Nation principle might be turned on the Great Powers. Just as gunboat diplomacy had wedged concessions in colonial markets for the Europeans, agreeing to the Japanese anti-racism clause risked a flood of unwelcome immigration, not just from Japanese allies, but from every other race. At a time when Billy Hughes joked about 'cannibals' and David Lloyd George spoke of 'niggers', it is possible that the Japanese had underestimated the potential impact, particularly on the British Empire, of a deceptively simple issue.

Saionji sent Makino and Chinda, his two heavy hitters, to meet with House, to press upon him the fact that racial equality was implicit in the rhetoric of most, if not all of the delegates before they reached the Conference. House conceded that some statement of equality was in keeping with the broad, internationalist aims of the League, and tried to draft something non-committal. The US Constitution, after all, boldly asserted that all men were created equal, but was still able to exclude non-white races from many aspects of its society. House hoped for something similarly toothless, but faced strong pressure, both from the Japanese, who wanted something specific, and from the Australians, who didn't want anything about equality at all. He even went so far as to show Balfour a note based on the American Declaration of Independence, in the vain hope that it might get him to agree on language. Considering the nation at which the Declaration of Independence had originally been intended as a polemic, it was perhaps naïve to expect much agreement from Balfour.

'Mr Balfour said that was an eighteenth century proposition which he did not believe was true. He believed that it was true in a certain sense that all men of a particular nation were created equal, but not that a man of Central Africa was created equal to a European.'[7]

On 13 February, Makino tried a different tack. At the Commission of the League of Nations, he tabled an amendment to a clause in the pre-existing Article 21 on 'religious liberty', which already established that no member state would be able to persecute someone for their beliefs. Makino proposed that the following words be added to the clause: 'The equality of nations being a basic principle of the League of Nations, the High Contracting Parties agree to accord, as soon as possible, to all alien nationals of States members of the League equal and just treatment in every respect, making no distinction, either in law or in fact, on account of their race or nationality.'[8]

Makino had called the other delegates' bluff. Were they a united, liberal community or not? The British delegate, Robert Cecil, stated that the racial equality clause had unpleasant implications for the organisation of the British Empire, and suggested the motion should be postponed, pending further discussion. Other delegates pounced, revealing objections to the original religious clause that they had not previously voiced. For the Greek statesman Eleftherios Venizelos, doubtless thinking of the millions of Turkish Muslims both in and near his territory, a statement of religious liberty was itself problematic – instead, he proposed that the entire clause, original, amendment and all, be dropped. This only irked the Portuguese, who had been rather hoping that the treaty would add a clause calling on divine authority – sure to create entire new points of argument between Christian denominations, not to mention the implied exclusion of Buddhists, Shintoists and any other believers who did not share Portugal's Catholic sentiments. If Makino had hoped to sneak the clause in, he had instead created enough of a disagreement to guarantee that it would be postponed for further debate.

Wilson left the next day for America, giving all parties a brief breathing-space. Makino and Chinda tried to put their case to Billy Hughes, in what was evidently an unpleasant meeting for all – the Japanese noblemen thought the gruff Australian to be uncouth and rude, while Hughes found their entreaties smarmy and obsequious. Despite this, Hughes was ready to negotiate, and offered to withdraw his opposition if the proposed amendment was not allowed to influence pre-existing immigration policies.

By 11 April, when Makino next raised the subject, the language of the clause had been substantially softened, and called simply for 'the principle of equality of nations and just treatment of their nationals'. Since this was only a principle, and not a statement with a particular legal force, it was greeted with support from other delegates, including the French, Italians, Czechs and even the Chinese. A shamefaced Robert Cecil announced he was unable to support it.

As the chairman, Wilson tried to dissuade the Japanese. As a sitting President of the United States, he could not support an idea that, however vague, was sure to lead to further debates on race, and hence cost him vital votes in California. He also suggested that the League itself might be undermined by the presence of such a clause. Wilson's attitude towards the Japanese remained kindly, if patronising – he clearly believed that they had not fully thought through the implications of their proposal for some of the other nations. Regardless, Wilson seemed similarly unaware of the pressure that the Japanese were under. Saionji's team had no choice but to push for the clause – to save face back home, they had to be seen to have done their best. If Saionji was to return home without it, he needed to be able to show that he had given it his all, only to be defeated by other interests.

'The Japanese told me with all oriental courtesy,' said a worried Wilson to Clemenceau and Lloyd George, 'that, if we didn't take their side on this article of the treaty, they couldn't sign the rest.'[9]

The impasse reached its climax on 28 April 1919, when Makino insisted on putting it to a vote. Not a single negative vote was recorded, instead the Japanese proposal gained the public support of France, Italy, China, Serbia, Greece and Czechoslovakia – a total of 11 votes of the 17 available.

The remaining six votes were not registered, split between the United States, Great Britain, Portugal, Romania and the absent Belgium.

Wilson's reaction, much to the chagrin of Peace Conference apologists, was to damn the League of Nations in the eyes of the Japanese. He ruled that although there was a majority vote in favour of the motion, there were clearly strong objections to it from other quarters. Consequently, the motion would not carry. A 'broken-hearted' Makino reported the incident to his own press corps, and the news soon reached Japan:

> The Japanese told me with all oriental courtesy that, if we didn't take their side on this article of the treaty [racial equality], they couldn't sign the rest.
> WOODROW WILSON

'Led by the United States, all six major powers opposed the racial equality clause in the Commission. America thinks that this proposition and her own so-called Japanese immigration question are too closely related. That is, if the League of Nations nullifies racial or colour lines, the American refusal to allow [Japanese] to enter that country will be considered unfair, and under international pressure she may be finally forced to abandon her attitude towards Orientals ... On the merits of our achievements during the World War, we deserve equal treatment from the others. Also, if one of the Allies' most popular slogans, "A World Safe for Democracy", is to be carried into serious practice, the subjects of member-nations must be accorded equal and just treatment, without any discrimination against either race or nationality – or religion. If the League of Nations fails in this fundamental principle, she will not be able to adjust difficulties between member nations of different colours and will automatically lose prestige.' [10]

Far from hearing the Japanese point of view, promoting the cause of international harmony, or valuing a democratic majority, Wilson had slapped down a majority vote using a bizarre pretext, asserting instead the status quo as maintained by the British and Americans. For all his lack of tact, Konoe Fumimaro had been proved right – the new order was an Anglo-American-centred peace.

11

The Shandong Question

Of far greater importance, and controversy, to the Conference as a whole was Japan's territorial claim over the Shandong peninsula. Like the Pacific islands, it had been seized from the Germans in the war, but the Germans had only leased the territory from the Chinese. The thorny issue presented to the Conference was whether the peninsula should be restored to its rightful owners, the Chinese, or handed as a spoil of war to its occupiers, the Japanese.

Shandong was vital to the Japanese. It gave them a foothold in China and a railway line into the heart of Asia, along with valuable mining rights. It was, however, also a point of honour with the Chinese, and perilously close to Beijing. China itself was in a state of great unrest after the abdication of the Last Emperor, with warlordism rampant and great disagreement over who was in charge. These rivalries extended even to the delegation itself, whose nominal leader was ineffectual, and whose underlings represented conflicting power blocs back home. China had one man able to fight for its interests in the form of Wellington Koo (1888–1985), soon promoted to the *de facto* leadership of its delegation. One of the first products of China's belated attempts to catch up with the West, the youthful Koo had been educated in the United States and was on friendly terms with Woodrow Wilson. He spoke excellent English, had an encyclopaedic knowledge of legal precedents in European treaties, and had the debating skills sufficient to put them all to use. The first 'modern' Chinese on the international scene, Koo dazzled the Conference with his eloquent appeals, and presented a serious threat to the Japanese position.

Japan had only limited items in its favour: Saionji's own personal contacts, the concession already made over racial equality, and the unavoidable fact that the Chinese government, or rather, one of the two rival Chinese governments, had already assented to the handover of Shandong in the wake of the Twenty-One Demands. One final boon, which the Japanese did their best to exploit, was the lack of interest displayed by many of the other Conference delegates, who regarded a scrap of land on the other side of the world as being of little importance. Hence, the issue only cropped up on three occasions during the Conference, presenting the Chinese with only three opportunities to press their own case, often to a disinterested audience, many of whom had their eyes on the clock and their minds on lunch.

On the morning of 27 January 1919, Makino read a prepared statement to the Conference, in which he outlined Japan's wish for the Pacific islands, and the Shandong Peninsula. In all cases, he argued, Japan regarded these territories as its rightful acquisition, in payment for sacrifices made during the war, particularly for the hard-fought conquest of the Shandong city of Jiaozhou (Kiaochow).

Wellington Koo had only a day to come up with a response, and delivered it the following day; it was his first speech to the international community and deeply impressed many delegates.

'China was fully cognizant of the services rendered to her by the heroic army and navy of Japan in rooting out German power from Shandong,' said Koo. But China was grateful to a number of Allied powers, including Great Britain, without whose presence in the region, Koo strongly implied, the Japanese might have seized more than just Shandong. 'China appreciated these services all the more,' he added with impressively Occidental-style sarcasm, 'because her people in Shandong had also suffered and sacrificed in connection with the military operations for the capture of [Jiaozhou], especially in regard to requisitions for labour and supplies of all kinds.' The implication was clear – far from being rescued from imperialist aggression, Shandong had simply swapped one group of oppressive invaders for another, and unless the Conference acted, the Japanese conquest would be ratified by an organisation sworn to proceed through 'open covenants openly arrived at'.

Grateful as they were for such 'assistance', Koo said: 'the Chinese delegation felt that they would be false to their duty to China and to the world if they did not object to paying their debts of gratitude by selling the birthright of their countrymen and thereby sowing the seeds of discord for the future.'[1]

Tokyo had made its position known to Saionji already – if Japan did not get to keep Shandong, Saionji was to refuse to sign both the Peace Treaty and the League Covenant. Expecting trouble from his underlings, Saionji hatched a plan to face the Conference on his own, later confessing: *During the Paris Peace Conference, when the Shandong issue became the subject of heated discussion, I determined to send back all the other delegates, since they were too troublesome, and to remain alone to settle the matter.* Reading between the lines, Saionji intended to sacrifice Shandong if necessary and sign the Treaty regardless, placing his personal belief in international-ism above the temporal demands of the Japanese government. This led to frank exchanges with the likes of Konoe, determined to follow Tokyo's order to the letter. Saionji stood firm, informing his underlings that there were issues of greater importance than a piece of land in China, and if they disagreed with him, they were free to leave Paris.[2]

> When the Shandong issue became the subject of heated discussion, I determined to send back all the other delegates, since they were too troublesome, and to remain alone to settle the matter.
>
> SAIONJI KINMOCHI

'They are not bluffers,' said Wilson, 'and they will go home unless we give them what they should not have.'[3]

On the record, it was Makino who was presenting the case for Japan – in fact, Saionji did not arrive until early March, leaving the responsibility for the entire January meeting with Makino, Chinda and Matsui. But with the Shandong ques-tion off the table for February, Saionji arrived in time to call in every available favour. He went to see his old friend Clem-enceau, and impressed upon the French leader that, despite the bluster of China's delegation, the Chinese had already agreed to hand over German rights in Shandong to the Japa-nese long ago.

The next time the subject of Shandong came up, Clem-enceau was ready to interrupt Lansing at a meeting of Foreign Ministers, and to describe his conversation with Saionji. Clemenceau, too, drew on Saionji's Parisian links, and told the assembled delegates that he had known him since his student days, and that when Saionji assured him that the Japanese fully intended to return Shandong to China, he was ready to believe him.

On 22 April, Wilson apologised to the Chinese delegates in a private meeting at his house. His difficulty, he admitted, was that the secret treaties between China and Japan, and Japan and Britain and France, had entirely muddied the waters. In particular, he mentioned an exchange of notes between China and Japan in September 1918 following the Nishihara Loans, when the Chinese minister in Tokyo had gone on the record with: 'the Chinese government was pleased to agree to the above-mentioned articles proposed by the Japanese government'. Wellington Koo argued that the entire exchange was only made under duress, as with the Twenty-One Demands in 1915. But China's prospects did not look good – Koo could hardly argue that the Chinese did not accept the Japanese presence in Shandong, when only four months earlier, his government had been publicly granting further concessions to the Japanese there.[4]

An impatient Lloyd George told Koo to make up his mind: 'Which would China prefer – to allow Japan to succeed to the German rights in Shandong as stated in the treaty between China and Germany, or to recognize Japan's position in Shandong as stipulated in the treaties between China and Japan?' Clemenceau was also present, and remained tacitly on Saionji's side, refusing to add anything more than his brusque agreement with whatever Lloyd George said.[5]

Saionji may have had one further bargaining chip, which he held in reserve until the end of April. Makino ensured that the subject of the racial equality clause was mentioned one further time, albeit in passing. The issue hung like a shadow over the final days of negotiations, and Wilson feared it would be reintroduced just as the Treaty was being ratified, which would force America itself to refuse to sign.[6]

Wilson caved in – he had slapped down the Japanese over the crucial racial equality issue, and knew that they were unlikely to be appeased with a handful of Pacific islands. Concluding that it was in the League's longer-term interests to uphold a bad treaty rather than to tear one up, he granted the Japanese demands for Shandong, on the condition that Japan made a separate declaration concerning its good intentions. Makino was swift to oblige:

'The policy of Japan is to hand back the Shandong Peninsula in full sovereignty to China retaining only the economic privileges granted to Germany and the right to establish a settlement under the usual conditions at [Qingdao]. The owners of the Railway will use specific Police only to ensure security for traffic. They will be used for no other purpose. The Police Force will be composed of Chinese, and such Japanese instructors as the Directors of the Railway may select will be appointed by the Chinese government.'[7]

The fates of millions of people now hung on the promises of Saionji and Makino themselves backed only by the personal assurances of Clemenceau, and it was plain to many that it might not be enough. 'Baron Makino has given his word of honor,' wrote Bonsal, 'that the withdrawal from Shandong will be carried out as soon as it can be done with dignity, and there is no one here whose honor is held in higher esteem than his. But this is not a personal matter. It is an international problem of far-reaching importance. Makino may be disavowed by his Emperor, the son of the Sun Goddess, or he may be thrown out and his commitment disavowed by the Diet. None too cheerfully, it has been decided to incur these obvious dangers.'

Despite Japanese assurances, Wilson fretted sufficiently about the decision to lose sleep over it that night. The following morning, he told Ray Baker: 'The only hope was to unite the world together, get the League of Nations with Japan in it, and then try to secure justice for the Chinese.' Otherwise, he feared,

> China was offered up as a sacrifice to propitiate the threatening Moloch of Japan.
> ROBERT LANSING

the Japanese might walk out of the Conference, and join with the Russians and the Germans to create an all-new Axis.

In his own diaries, Lansing conceded: '[the] President fully believed that the League of Nations was in jeopardy, and that to save it he was compelled to subordinate every other consideration. The result was that China was offered up as a sacrifice to propitiate the threatening Moloch of Japan.'[8]

The Conference ended with the Japanese making great colonial gains in the Far East. The putative limitations of the 999-year leases were mere marks on paper as far as Japanese patriots were concerned. The loss of the racial equality clause was a disappointment, but its sacrifice may have been the vital element that gained them Shandong.

However, the compromise offered by Saionji and Makino managed to displease all parties equally – the Chinese were to regard the subsequent Japanese withdrawal from Shandong as too slow, while the Japanese were annoyed that there was any semblance of a withdrawal at all. Saionji himself was keener to stress that the Conference had seen an internationalist Japan participating on the world stage. *Amongst those provisions which should form the basis of a lasting peace*, he wrote, *the most notable are the League of Nations and the Labour Convention. The League Covenant, which forms the core of the Peace Treaty, aims to avoid war through the power of co-operation between all nations, and will deal with all international problems.*

Glossing over the snubs, exclusions and attacks of his months in Paris, he tried to impress on Tokyo the significance of the Conference:

The results of the recent conference will have a profound effect on the position of Japan in international politics. Japan has joined the ranks of the five great powers and this is the beginning of our participation in European politics. Furthermore, since we occupy an important place in the League of Nations, we have acquired the right to participate generally in future in all East-West matters.[9]

In his final years Prince Kinmochi Saionji was a much respected former prime minister and elder statesman. Here he is consulted by the Japanese Cabinet over the situation in Manchuria. The Japanese occupation of the region in 1931 had provoked an angry reaction from China.

III

The Legacy

12

The Dark Valley

Saionji came home via the United Kingdom, where he dined with King George V and explained the diplomatic give-and-take that had required him to support the Kaiser's trial. Some of the other Japanese delegates took their time returning, including Konoe, who toured his father's old haunts in Germany before taking a leisurely trip back through the UK and USA. Konoe arrived back in Japan full of admiration for the way of life in foreign countries, and wrote several negative pieces about Japan that led some readers to assume that he was thinking of emigrating. He also wrote a sharply critical article about the Peace Conference, which he called 'the end of idealism'. Even as Saionji pleaded with his superiors to see the positive side of Paris, Konoe regarded the Conference as little more than a confirmation of his doubts, with Anglo-American interests shoved through, while the demands of lesser nations like Japan were ignored.[1]

Saionji continued to regard Konoe as his protégé, and expressed his hope on many occasions that the ill-informed youth would mature into someone with a more statesman-like demeanour. But like the young Saionji, Konoe's noble privileges afforded him a meteoric rise to a position of authority, and by December 1921 he had been elected acting president of the Imperial Diet. The following year, Saionji still expressed hope that Konoe was growing up: *I understand that some people suspected him of harbouring dangerous leftist thoughts. But he is no fool, and of late he seems to be behaving quite prudently.*[2]

But Konoe was no internationalist. Paris had only confirmed his suspicions about the rest of the world, and he drifted ever closer to a militarist faction within the Japanese government. Konoe came to regard Saionji as the 'citadel' that protected parliamentary government in Japan, but his use of the term was not that of a fellow defender, but of an enemy preparing to attack.

Saionji was thrown into domestic trouble-shooting as soon as he was back in Japan. One of his first acts after returning from Paris was to attend the going-away party for the newly appointed Governor-General of the Korean colony – a replacement for the discredited official who had presided over the atrocities towards the March 1st Movement. Raising his glass and calling for silence, Saionji pointedly proposed a toast: *May Your Excellency have an enlightened and civilized administration.*[3]

Meanwhile, the Taishō Emperor, plagued by ill health throughout his life, was now truly unfit to rule, and it was agreed that his son Hirohito should become Prince Regent. This, surprisingly, was a relatively easy matter, as it was already allowed for within the Meiji Constitution – perhaps the European influences of its authors allowed for troublesome rulers in a manner that an exclusively Japanese document might have been afraid to admit. Saionji was more concerned with a deceptively minor issue that had much more drastic implications. The Regent, Hirohito, had selected a distant cousin as his bride, who unhelpfully turned out to be colour-blind. Princess Nagako was a Satsuma woman, and when the news somehow got out that the administration was blocking her betrothal, protests in Japan started to form along the old lines of the civil war stand-off. The argument re-ignited Satsuma and Chōshū sentiments within the government, and placed Saionji under serious pressure, as he enjoyed many links with Satsuma powerbrokers – not the least Baron Makino, who was now Imperial Household Minister.

Saionji did his best to make virtues out of vices. Hirohito's education had been in the hands of the venerable Admiral Tōgō Heihachirō, who was highly respected but a military man nonetheless. Saionji pleaded with the Empress for several months, finally securing her consent to send Hirohito out of the country. He packed the Crown Prince off to Europe for a study trip, where he hoped that encounters with European nobility might encourage the future Emperor to share his interest in the League of Nations. It was the first time an Imperial heir had studied abroad, and itself established a lasting precedent – Hirohito's son and grandson would both study at Oxford. While Prince Hirohito hobnobbed with royalty (developing, in the process, a lifelong love of English breakfasts), Saionji was free to resolve the paperwork over the Regency, and to deal with the betrothal issue. Saionji, familiar from his European days with the perils of congenital defects in royal families, opposed the knowing introduction of a congenital defect into the Imperial family, not the least because colour-blindness blocked a Japanese man from military service, and any imperial heir was obliged to serve a period in the armed forces.

In the end, Saionji was defeated when the bride's father argued that his daughter was not really colour-blind at all, but merely colour-*weak*. The marriage went ahead, but its implications impressed upon many of the commoner members of the Diet that the Imperial Household was a truly different world. The impasse had cost at least one life (Prime Minister Hara was murdered by a railway worker in November 1921), and despite his defeat, Saionji was established as the ideal man to deal with matters between the monarch and the parliament. In one of his last diary entries, the ill-fated Hara summed up his fellow politicians' position: 'It is probably true … that Saionji, whose family has had an unbroken relationship with the Crown for several hundred years, is different from ourselves.' [4]

During the Regency period, Saionji and his constitutional monarchists dominated court affairs. As one of only three surviving *genrō*, he was a strong influence on the selection of a prime minister to replace the murdered Hara – true to form, he honourably nominated someone who was not in his own party. He also refused to reward a political assassination with a change in government, encouraging Hara's successor to work with the pre-existing cabinet. He maintained a similar stance through the negotiations over half a dozen successive governments in the 1920s, during which period he was also promoted in the nobility to the rank of Prince.

However, although the 1920s were to a certain extent the apogee of Saionji's power in the Japanese government, they also saw the rise of the faction that would supersede him.

The catalyst came, unsurprisingly, from China. The warlord Zhang Zuolin, who ruled what was left of Manchuria after the Japanese lease of the Liaodong area, enjoyed ever-growing powers. He captured Beijing in 1926 and briefly proclaimed himself the Grand Marshall of China – a direct challenge to Chiang Kai-shek in the south. Thanks to their control over the 'pincers' of Liaodong and Shandong, the Japanese had no difficulty landing troops in Tianjin, and warned Zhang that it was in his best interests to withdraw. On 18 September 1931, in precisely the sort of action that both Saionji and the Chinese had long feared, the Japanese army guarding the South Manchurian railway used its position to plant a bomb on one of its own bridges. The device was detonated as Zhang Zuolin's train passed beneath the bridge and the Japanese-owned railway above it – fatally injuring the warlord.

It was immediately assumed, as in the case of the assassination of Queen Min a generation earlier, that the Japanese government was behind it. But neither the Army nor Navy Ministers knew of the plans for the incident – in fact, the death of Zhang, who had enjoyed good relations with the Japanese, substantially *damaged* Japanese interests in Manchuria. Presuming junior officers were responsible, Saionji pressed for a purge of insubordinate elements in the military: *If it becomes evident that the Japanese Army was responsible, then discipline must be enforced through strict punishment. Even if public feeling towards China should suffer for a time, proper retribution would enhance our national credibility and the honour of both the Japanese Army and the nation. It would also restore the trust in the Japanese army which we have seen lacking in the past.*[5]

Fearing tacit support for the army, even among other courtiers, Saionji instructed Prime Minister Tanaka Giichi to report his suspicions directly to the Emperor. Tanaka, however, failed to do so, and also failed to adequately bring the perpetrators of the bombing to book. Both among the public and, crucially, among the army itself, Tokyo was seen to secretly support the bombers, which would soon lead to further acts of terrorism.

Saionji experienced similar belligerence in his dealings with the Japanese navy, whose representatives insisted on a rise in the ratio of Japanese ships to those in the navies of the US and Britain at the London Naval Conference. Saionji's response displays his continued insistence on diplomatic consensus, and his exasperation with the armed forces, whose sense of entitlement and demanding attitude reflected a move from an internationalist Japan to an autonomous, grasping state: *For Navy partisans to insist on a 70 per cent ratio and to clamour that our delegates should kick over their seats, leave the conference and come home if there is the slightest diminution ... would be a most serious mistake ... [W]hen the matter is judged from the wider viewpoints of politics and diplomacy, [the Navy] cannot hope for complete victory ... . The strength that derives from reckless plans and emergency ad hoc preparations is virtually no strength at all ... Japan should lead other nations to recognise her earnest promotion of international peace by voluntarily accepting 60 per cent.*[6]

Saionji's nemeses in these negotiations were Fleet Admiral Tōgō and Prince Fushimi, who were determined to push the size of the Japanese fleet upwards in relation to the US and British navies. After all, who was going to enforce it if they disobeyed? Despite Wilson's diplomacies and entreaties at the Paris Peace Conference, the United States Congress had failed to ratify the League of Nations covenant, leaving the international peacemaking body almost entirely toothless. Without America, the League could not maintain a firm stance on military action or punitive sanctions. Without the League, the increasingly isolationist US was unlikely to interfere in foreign affairs.

But Saionji's efforts over the treaty found his powers eroded. The Privy Council's vice-president, Hiranuma, took steps to exclude Ministers of State from meetings of a sub-committee, leading Saionji to comment on the dangerous precedent: *This disturbs me very much, for it is only the latest in a long series of flaws ... .*[7] Although Saionji got his way with the London Naval Treaty, it was truly a 'fragile victory'. He had overcome opposition from members of the Court, the government, the nobility and the Privy Council; he was now 80 years old and his younger foes were gaining ground.

Matters worsened in 1931. A militarist faction attempted to take matters into its own hands, with young officers in the Sakura-kai (Cherry Blossom Society) plotting a *coup d'état* in March – cherry blossom season. Their plot involved a series of manufactured riots and terrorist incidents, during which they expected the Army Minister, General Ugaki, to mobilise troops in their support. This was news to General Ugaki, or so at least he would later claim, when the promised crowds of supporters failed to show up. Another Prime Minister fell victim to an assassin, seemingly in direct reaction to the London Naval Treaty. But the worst damage of all would come, as ever, from China.

Fleet Admiral Fushimi Hiroyasu (1875–1946) was a cousin of the Emperor and, coincidentally, a son-in-law of the last Shōgun, Tokugawa Yoshinobu. A lifelong navy man, he studied in both Germany and Britain, and was a strong opponent of the Washington Naval Agreement. He was appointed naval Chief of Staff in 1932, and remained in the post until 1941.

Saionji and his supporters were alerted to a number of skirmishes in Manchuria and Korea. Fearing that junior officers were once again preparing to manufacture an excuse for a military escalation in Manchuria, Saionji moved quickly to gain Imperial support. His reasoning was based on his own youthful experience – the rhetoric of the rebellious officers, whenever it surfaced, had echoes of the Meiji Restoration, in which rebels had claimed their allegiance was to the desires of an Emperor whose true wishes were being kept from his subjects. Even as it had modernised Japan, the Meiji Restoration had hence set a dangerous precedent for a new generation: that disobedience and rebellion could be presented as an act of loyalty to the throne.

Saionji saw to it that the Emperor made his feelings on the matter crystal clear. Minami, the new Army Minister, was summoned to an audience with Hirohito and ordered to maintain strict discipline, particularly over the formation of political groups among young officers. Saionji met with Minami later to hammer the point home: *It is extremely bad to be sending villains and roughnecks and members of rightwing terrorist groups to Manchuria. That the army should make use of such people is bad for national and army prestige alike. If the army incites these people then the reputation of the Japanese military abroad will be no better than theirs ... Manchuria and Mongolia are Chinese territory and anything to do with Chinese diplomacy must be left to the Foreign Ministry.*[8]

But he was too late. A group of officers at Mukden (Shenyang) in Manchuria had been planning something all year. On 18 September 1931, a bomb exploded near a Japanese-owned railway track in Manchuria, only a few hundred metres from one of Zhang Xueliang's bases. The damage was minimal – not even sufficient to prevent the passage of a train only ten minutes later, which simply wobbled a little on a slightly damaged track. However, the incident was reported in the Japanese press as a significant attack, to which the Japanese army responded with extreme force the next day.[9]

The 'swimming pool' at the local Japanese officers' club

turned out to be a bunker concealing two artillery pieces, which opened fire on the Chinese base in 'retaliation' on 19 September. The inexperienced Chinese forces scattered, and by the end of the day, the Japanese army was in control of the Manchurian capital.

Back in Tokyo, Saionji immediately went into action. His own very limited resources extended no further than the Court itself, and he implemented what measures he could. Saionji knew very well the means by which a resignation could be used to further a cause – he had used the method himself in the old deadlock over the *Eastern Liberal News*. A resignation by the incumbent government would leave the Army's actions unpunished and unmonitored, and force a successor administration to deal with the invasion of Manchuria as a *fait accompli*. Consequently, Saionji made sure that the Lord Keeper of the Privy Seal understood that the Emperor was not to accept the government's resignation. Furthermore, if a representative of the military reported the Manchurian troop movements to the Emperor, the Emperor should respond neither with silence nor acceptance, but with a stern warning that he would consider the matter.

The Manchurian Incident was Saionji's effective defeat. He was unable to stop the Japanese troops in Korea from coming to the aid of their comrades in Manchuria, which involved the illegal crossing of a national border. Controversially, the cabinet authorised supply lines to the illegally invading troops, not because it necessarily approved of their action, but because it feared public sentiment would force its resignation anyway. The Japanese press was already reporting the Manchurian Incident as a bold defence against overwhelming odds, talking up both the extent of the original bombing and the strength of the Chinese enemy.

Some of Saionji's faction within the cabinet suggested that it was time to put the military on the spot. The army's leaders, it was argued, should be forced to stand in front of the Emperor and explain matters both to him and to the Prime Minister whose will they had disobeyed. Impressively, the Emperor appeared to agree. Hirohito fretted that the Manchurian Incident was sure to achieve what no other act had previously managed: to unite both America and the League of Nations in censure sufficient to lead to sanctions against Japan. Saionji, however, rushed to Tokyo to prevent the meeting taking place. *My duty today*, he said to Shidehara, *is twofold, to avoid damaging the spirit of the Constitution granted by the Meiji Emperor, and to observe international treaties.* Saionji had not been shy of using the Emperor's influence in the past, but only where it was sure to go unopposed. His concern with the Manchurian Incident was not only that it would set a dangerous precedent for the involvement of the throne in political matters, but the terrifying prospect that the Emperor might one day give a command that his army would disobey.[10]

The military had won, not only in Manchuria and Tokyo, but also against the League of Nations. Although the Chinese lodged a complaint on the first day of hostilities, the League took over a month to pass a resolution calling for the Japanese to withdraw from Manchuria. Meanwhile, the Chinese president Chiang Kai-shek was forced to resign over the incident, as was his successor when Chinese troops failed to hold a new line against the Japanese advance.

As predicted, the invasion of Manchuria was criticised by both the United States and the League of Nations. In February 1932, Japan unilaterally recognised the newly formed state of Manchuria (Manchukuo), a Japanese puppet regime nominally ruled by Puyi, the former Last Emperor of China, whose ancestors came from Manchuria. The League refused to recognise the state, and Japan withdrew from the League.

Saionji fumed that the younger politicians had entirely forgotten the ideals of their forebears. He bitterly opposed Japan's exit from the League, warning other politicians that leaving it was a worthless gesture – there would still be sanctions from League states after all, and now it would be even harder to undo the damage.

> What we aimed at was Japan in the World. The problems of the Far East can be better resolved through co-operation with England and America ...
>
> SAIONJI KINMOCHI

Meanwhile, the military faction was using the rhetoric of expelling the influence of white powers, an 'Asian Monroe Doctrine', as an excuse for invading China.

As I said ... the reason that Japan maintains her world power status is that she holds the baton of command with England and America. If Japan loses her grip like France and Italy, how will she develop as a world power? In the past, when Itō [Hirobumi] and myself and others thought about Japan's future path, we never thought in terms of anything so narrow as ... an 'Asian Monroe Doctrine'. What we aimed at was Japan in the World. The problems of the Far East can be better resolved through co-operation with England and America ... .[11]

Saionji's use of 'Japan in the World' was a forlorn gesture towards the past, an evocation of the magazine he published 35 years previously, with all its hope of international co-operation. But even in 1896, *Japan in the World* had been a reactive gesture. As Saionji faced his twilight years, Japan itself seemed to be entering a dark valley of rising militarism and increasing ostracism on the world stage. In February 1932,

Saionji told Konoe that he had had enough. He wanted to resign his position as a *genrō*, fearing that before long he would be asked to 'select' a new Prime Minister from a list of candidates comprised solely of military men.

13
Last of the *Genrō*

Before Saionji could officially resign, Japan lost another Prime Minister to political assassination. Inukai Tsuyoshi had inherited a chaotic cabinet, an economy in crisis, and an international incident in China. Waylaid by a gang of naval officers barely out of their teens, he tried to talk his way out of the situation.

'Dialogue is useless,' said one of them, and killed him. The murder was another attempt at a *coup* like that of the earlier Sakura-kai, but despite the deaths, it similarly failed to ignite a full-scale revolution. Other insurgents attacked Makino's house, and there was a similar assault on Saionji's office, which came to nothing. The 11 ringleaders then turned themselves in, leading to an embarrassing courtroom drama, in which, just as Saionji had feared, they aired their claims to a supportive audience that they were not rebels but *loyalists*, serving the perceived will of a Emperor who had been misled by his courtiers.

Soon afterwards, Konoe Fumimaro met with Saionji and made a bold suggestion – far from clinging to parliamentary democracy, Saionji should let the military have their way.

Dump the government in their hands, where they were sure to bungle things sufficiently to ruin their popular support. But even if Saionji were to agree with the plan, which he thought was one of Konoe's silliest, 'the military' was not a single unified body. Although the interests of the army and navy were broadly in opposition to liberals like Saionji, there was no single military faction, but a number of interest groups, jockeying for position among themselves. The government could neutralise one faction, through replacement of officers or a judicious reposting, but that would only remove one threat of many. Saionji faced not merely military interests determined to extend Japanese imperialism in Asia, but military groups who could not agree on how. One faction, largely rooted in the army, favoured a 'Strike North' strategy, using Manchuria as a base to expand into Russia. Another, largely rooted in the navy, favoured a 'Strike South' strategy, using Taiwan as a base to expand into South-East Asia.

Saionji refused on principle, but as he had predicted, the only viable candidate to replace the murdered Inukai was a military man, Admiral Saitō Makoto. An ally of Saionji, Saitō was that same Governor-General of Korea who he had so conspicuously toasted a decade earlier in 1919, but even so, naval officers had killed the Prime Minister, and now the court itself was obliged to put a navy man in the vacated position.[1]

A series of short-lived administrations followed that of Saitō, while the position of the Emperor hovered on the brink of constitutional crisis. Saionji refused to nominate any new *genrō* to replace him, hoping instead to create a new advisory body that could prevent less scrupulous successors from abusing the responsibility. He commented that he regarded the Constitution as already half-abandoned by the military, and that with his options running low, he could only hope to delay their rise to power. Although Saionji already seemed to consider the battle lost, he hoped to prevent a violent and sudden change in power – unable to pursue his beloved internationalism, he chose instead to shore up the imperial institution.

The right wing smeared Saionji in a muck-raking pamphlet. His association with Émile Acollas was dragged up, and used to imply that he had Communist sympathies, as was his decade spent living in 'revolutionary France' and his editorship of the 'radical' *Eastern Liberal News*.

The violent revolt Saionji had been dreading came on the snowy morning of 26 February 1936 – it was, at the very least, the third plot against his group in 12 months, but the first to go into full action. A series of murders in Tokyo did away with the Finance Minister, the reasonable Admiral Saitō and the Inspector General of Military Education. Other assassination attempts were unsuccessful. Some 1,400 junior officers, mainly from the army, seized the centre of Tokyo. Despite being urged to flee by his staff, Saionji refused to leave his country house, determined to remain close to a telephone in case the Emperor needed him. In fact, it is unlikely that Saionji was ever in any immediate danger. He was worth far more to the rebels alive, as his presence in Tokyo could be used to gain support for an entirely military cabinet.

Far from staying out of 'political' decisions, Hirohito was livid. He openly called the rebels 'insurgents' and assured them they were directly contravening his orders. Nor was he prepared to listen to the standard excuse that the rebels were acting out of a sense of loyalty to him. Hirohito, presumably with Saionji's unhappy agreement by telephone, issued a proclamation that the rebels were traitors to the throne, and ordered the army proper to put down the uprising. Unwilling to attack their own, the army spent a day circulating the imperial edict, which was sufficient to persuade many of the rebels to sneak away. Two ringleaders committed ritual suicide in protest, and in the aftermath 19 were executed and 70 imprisoned.

The February 26 Incident ('2–26'), as it is usually called, ended with months of martial law in the Japanese capital. Although the Prime Minister survived, he soon lost his position anyway. Tighter controls were imposed on both the media and civilian protests – even though the revolt was a failure, it still strengthened the military's hold on the population.

Hirohito's direct interference had dispelled the immediate danger – by obeying his orders, the common soldiers escaped punishment and defused the crisis – but Saionji fretted over the cost. If the Emperor were associated closely with Saionji's liberal group, then he risked becoming a target himself. Saionji voiced his very real fear that another military faction, seeing an enemy in their head of state, might seek to remove him and replace him with a more malleable successor. There were, he feared plenty of candidates – not least Hirohito's cousin, Prince Fushimi, the Navy Chief of Staff whose involvement with the revolt was still unknown, or Hirohito's brother Prince Chichibu, whose allegiances to right-wingers had long been suspected, and who had returned to the capital against Imperial orders during the uprising and had to be sternly confined under house arrest by Imperial agents. *It is probably not something which will happen in my lifetime*, said Saionji, *but … Japanese history has sometimes repeated itself and one can find a considerable number of examples where, urged on by hangers-on, a younger brother has killed an older brother in order to ascend to the Throne. Of course,*

*the Emperor's younger brothers are not discussing anything
of the sort ... However, if they were to be led astray by odd
characters within the Court, and were elements to emerge
which got up to I-don't-know-what ...*[2]

He was unable to bring himself to suggest specifics, adding
merely that the matter was of the utmost importance.

One of Saionji's last, futile acts was to recommend a Prime
Minister he hoped would stand up to the army: Konoe Fumimaro. Since Japan was no longer a member of the League of
Nations, the men had lost one of their main points of contention. But Saionji's protégé had not mellowed with age – in
fact, he had returned from a recent trip to America full of
stories of anti-Japanese sentiment. He had often defended
Japanese actions in Manchuria, and enjoyed support from
the military.

But Konoe would unsurprisingly disappoint Saionji,
drifting ever closer to military factions. Saionji was now an
ailing man in his eighties, plagued by lower back pain and
exhausted by decades of court infighting. His eyesight was
worsening, and he claimed that it was becoming difficult for
him to read Japanese text, and that in his old age he preferred the clearer words of French books – not the classics,
but 'modern works' like those of his old friends in the Goncourt set.[3] Although this may well have been true, it might
have been the last deception left in Saionji's exhausted box of
tricks – for a man who supposedly couldn't read any more,
he still took regular deliveries of Japanese policy documents.
Although seldom seen after 1937, the old statesman was still
consulted over cabinet appointments. Fully aware that his recommendations were falling on deaf ears, and often acknowl-
edging that the battle was already lost, he usually abstained.
He did, however, occasionally make his displeasure felt over

some choices – he conspicuously blocked a bid by Konoe to become the Lord Keeper of the Privy Seal, hoping thereby to keep army influence out of the court. He also raised his objection to the appointment of Konoe to the Prime Minister's job in 1940, but he was ignored. *There is nothing to do*, he said, *but hold one's tongue and watch the lay of the land. Within ten or twenty years, the atmosphere may change and more progressive politics appear, but at present there is absolutely no alternative but to endure it in silence.*[4]

> There is nothing to do but hold one's tongue and watch the lay of the land. Within ten or twenty years, the atmosphere may change and more progressive politics appear, but at present there is absolutely no alternative but to endure it in silence.
>
> SAIONJI KINMOCHI

Saionji died in 1940 – although he lived to see Konoe take Japan to all-out war in China in 1937, he was spared the sight of the Japanese fleet attacking Pearl Harbor, which occurred, in a moment of inadvertent historical irony, on his birthday. In the war that followed, the Pacific islands awarded to Japan by the Treaty of Versailles became famous battlegrounds – in direct contravention of the directives of the League of Nations, the Japanese navy had fortified them and used them as bases.

In the Second World War, which Saionji had spent the last 20 years of his life so assiduously trying to prevent, Japan lost all of her territorial gains of the imperialist era. Korea was freed, and its first government was formed from the organisation that was founded in 1919. The Pacific islands mandate was handed over to the American victors, and the last of the '999-year leases' came to an end in 1994, with the independence of Palau.

The military factions fought to the last. When Hirohito decided to surrender in 1945, the palace suffered one final attempted coup by soldiers acting out of 'loyalty' to him. Saionji's suspicions, that the imperial family wanted to replace Hirohito with someone more malleable, would get a final airing soon afterwards, when Hirohito's younger brother publicly urged him to abdicate, accept the blame for the war, and allow the imperial family to install a new regent until such time as the Crown Prince (now the Heisei Emperor) came of age.

Even in death, Saionji continued to defend the Emperor – the last decade of his life, as enshrined in thousands of pages of diaries by Harada Kumao, was used as a gargantuan piece of evidence in the International Military Tribunal for the Far East. Saionji's enduring victory is the preservation of the imperial institution. In a controversial decision by the Allied victors, Hirohito and other members of the imperial family were exonerated of war crimes, permitting the continuation of Saionji's beloved constitutional monarchy.

∞∞∞

Militarism in Japan was finally defeated, not by the liberal stand of the likes of Saionji, but by the fiat of the Allied conquerors, who wrote an offensively-capable military out of the Japanese constitution. Post-war Japan's armed forces are, at least on paper, solely for defence. For Saionji, Japan's great loss in the 20th century would be in the bittersweet arrival of the United Nations, the ultimate successor to the abortive League. An organisation with greater longevity than the League, the UN continues to push Saionji's own brand of international diplomacy. Japan, however, does not have a permanent seat on the UN Security Council – a legacy of sides chosen in the 1940s, enduring into the 21st century.

Saionji's opponents, we must concede, also had their points. The ghost of Konoe would not have been surprised by the about-face in the 1950s, when the supposedly demilitarised Japanese industrial system was retooled to support a United Nations war effort in Korea. Japan became the 'unsinkable aircraft carrier' for America in the Pacific theatre.

In more modern times, 'resource-poor' Japan, as Konoe called it, continues to rely on other countries for its fuel. The posting of Japanese troops outside Japan, even in non-belligerent roles, remains a highly sensitive issue both domestically and abroad. Consequently, in the Gulf Wars of the late 20th and early 21st century, Japan's contribution was largely financial – Konoe would have appreciated the irony of foreign soldiers upholding an Anglo-American peace, fighting to secure oil for Japanese industry. Agitation from foreign powers for Japan to play a more active role continues to impinge on the terms of the post-war constitution.

Several of Saionji's descendants were prominent figures in post-war Japan, in sectors that he would have recognised. Among his grandchildren, Saionji Fujio (1910–86) became a chairman of the Nissan Corporation, while Saionji Kinkazu (1906–93) graduated from Oxford and entered the Foreign Ministry. He was caught leaking sensitive information to the Soviet spy Richard Sorge in 1942 – only his noble privileges saved him from trial. After the war, he became the owner of the Senators baseball team, now known as the Hokkaidō Nippon Ham Fighters, and served as ambassador in China for more than a decade. Kinkazu's eldest son Kazuteru graduated from Beijing University and subsequently became the editor of one of Japan's largest newspapers, the *Asahi Shinbun*.

Meanwhile, the Konoe family stayed in politics. Konoe's grandson Hosokawa Morihiro was elected Prime Minister of Japan in 1993, and famously acknowledged that the Second World War had been 'a war of aggression, a mistaken war'. In doing so he broke four decades of silence over the issue from Japanese leaders, and acknowledged that his grandfather's mentor, the last *genrō*, might have been right all along.

Notes

Introduction

1. S Bonsal, *Suitors and Suppliants* (Prentice-Hall, New York: 1946) p 233.

2. B Ōmura, *The Last Genrō – Prince Saionji: The Man Who Westernized Japan* (J B Lippincott Company, Philadelphia: 1938), glosses over the status of Saionji's long-term mistress Okiku, calling her a 'wife' through most of his book, although he is unable to maintain this façade by the time Okiku leaves Saionji.

3. M MacMillan, *Paris 1919* (John Murray, London: 2001) p 310. MacMillan's endnotes for this passage cite several pages from 'Kumao' (i.e. Harada – she has confused his given name and surname) but none of them refer specifically to a mistress in Paris. Japanese sources are more forthcoming – Ōmura, *The Last Genrō*, p 351 names the woman as Ohana, as does K Harada, *Fragile Victory: Prince Saionji and the 1930 London Treaty Issue from the Memoirs of Baron Harada Kumao* (Wayne State University Press, Detroit: 1968) p 37. Saionji was also accompanied in Paris by his *daughter* Shinko and her husband – see, for example, the

photograph of the delegates reprinted in T Iwai, *Saionji Kinmochi: Saigo no Genrō* (Iwanami Shoten, Tokyo: 2003) p 143.

1: The Black Ships

1. Y Takekoshi, *Prince Saionji* (Ritsumeikan University, Kyoto: 1933) pp 15–16.
2. Ōmura, *The Last Genrō*, pp 16–17.
3. D Keene, *Emperor of Japan: Meiji and His World, 1852–1912* (Columbia University Press, New York: 2002) pp 14–22.
4. Takekoshi, *Prince Saionji*, pp 21–2.

2: Confused Loyalties

1. Takekoshi, *Prince Saionji*, p 28.
2. Keene, *Emperor of Japan*, p 75.
3. Keene, *Emperor of Japan*, pp 80–1. Ōmura, *The Last Genrō*, p 20, puts Saionji at the Emperor's side during the fight.
4. Keene, *Emperor of Japan*, pp 76, 78.
5. Keene, *Emperor of Japan*, p 85.

3: The Meiji Restoration

1. The reign title for the new Emperor was chosen to reflect the regime's hope for enlightened rule. It drew its meaning from a quotation of the ancient Chinese book of divination, the *Yi Jing* (I Ching): 'The sage, facing south, listens to the world. Facing the light (*mei*), he governs (*ji*).'
2. Keene, *Emperor of Japan*, p 124.
3. Takekoshi, *Prince Saionji*, p 42.
4. Takekoshi, *Prince Saionji*, p 43.

5. Iwai, *Saionji Kinmochi*, p 13.
6. Takekoshi, *Prince Saionji*, p 47. One is tempted to wonder, considering other misleading matters of protocol, if Saionji's generalship was only conferred on him *after* his successful mission, and that at the time of his setting out 'without time for ceremony', he was merely one of several courtiers assigned to the same task.
7. Takekoshi, *Prince Saionji*, p 54.
8. Takekoshi, *Prince Saionji*, p 50.
9. It is worth noting here that the use of the Emperor in this manner probably saved thousands of lives. Decades later, a similar tactic would be controversially used by the Allied Occupation forces – the preservation of Hirohito during the post-war transition probably saved even more.
10. Keene, *Emperor of Japan*, p 127.
11. Takekoshi, *Prince Saionji*, p 55.

4: Japonisme

1. Like the Meiji era itself, Ritsumeikan derived its name from a Chinese quotation – in this case, from the philosopher Mencius: 'Some die young, as some live long lives. This is decided by fate. Therefore, one's duty consists of cultivating one's mind during this mortal span and thereby establishing (*ritsu*) one's destiny (*mei*).' The *kan* simply refers to a hall or mansion.
2. Takekoshi, *Prince Saionji*, pp 75–6.
3. Harada, *Fragile Victory*, p 25.
4. Takekoshi, *Prince Saionji*, p 79.
5. Iwai, *Saionji Kinmochi*, p 23.
6. Iwai, *Saionji Kinmochi*, p 23.

7. Iwai, *Saionji Kinmochi*, p 23.
8. Takekoshi, *Prince Saionji*, p 81.
9. Iwai, *Saionji Kinmochi*, p 25.
10. Takekoshi, *Prince Saionji*, p 90.
11. Iwai, *Saionji Kinmochi*, pp 26–7. It is perhaps worth noting that Saionji appears to have completed three years of 'general studies', and was not included on the registry of the Paris Law School until 1875. In later years, he would claim to have a Bachelor of Laws from the Sorbonne, although it is likely that his certificate was actually a Diplôme d'Etudes Universitaires Générales. This is not necessarily a sign of deception – there was no direct translation available and no means of comparing the relative merits of degrees from one institution to another.
12. Takekoshi, *Prince Saionji*, p 85. That, at least, is how Takekoshi puts it, citing a dropout rate of between 80–90 per cent. It remains equally possible that most students were expecting little more than a grand tour of some 2–3 years, and returned home without dishonour.
13. C Nakae, *A Discourse by Three Drunkards on Government*, 1887 [trans. Nobuko Tsukui] (Weatherhill, New York: 1984).
14. G Clemenceau, *Grandeur and Misery of Victory* (George Harrap, London: 1930) p 140.
15. Ōmura, *The Last Genrō*, p 59. The same incident is repeated in Takekoshi, *Prince Saionji*, p 89, but in a confusing manner that suggested something has been lost in translation.
16. J Richardson, *Judith Gautier: A Biography* (Quartet Books, London: 1986) p 117. The book was republished as *La Soeur du Soleil* (*Sister of the Sun*) in 1887, shortly

before Gautier's critical success with *La Marchande de Sourires*. It is worth noting that there cannot have been many Japanese in London in the 1860s – the samurai Gautier met were undoubtedly in town for the Exhibition, although they may have been from Satsuma or the 'Kingdom of the Ryūkyū Islands' rather than Japan. The Chōshū Five, including Itō Hirobumi, would illegally leave Japan for Britain the following year.

17. Richardson, *Judith Gautier: A Biography*, pp 153–4; Takekoshi, *Prince Saionji*, p 87. Saionji's contribution is not clear; Japanese sources claim that he wrote the play with Gautier, and that he refused her offer of half the monies received. French sources note that the play existed as a puppetry performance sometime before its theatrical debut, and that the 1888 show was dedicated to Saionji. Richardson later claims, on p 176, that Gautier only had two Japanese friends, Saionji and 'Komiosi' (Kōmyōji). However, Takekoshi writes that Saionji was introduced to Gautier through their mutual friend Funakoshi Mamoru – which makes for at least one more Japanese in the circle. Ōmura, *The Last Genrō*, particularly pp 62, 67 and 98, insinuates that Kōmyōji had at least an unrequited crush or perhaps a clandestine affair with Gautier.

18. Takekoshi, *Prince Saionji*, p 91. Ōmura, *The Last Genrō*, p 64 repeats the same exchange, presumably using the same source as Takekoshi, and adds the parting phrase from Acollas: 'Don't quarrel with your destiny.'

5 : The Eastern Liberal News

1. To be fair, the pedestrian naming conventions may have been enforced humility, with no peasant wishing to

outperform his neighbours with a showy, patrician title like, say, *Saionji* – 'Temple of the Western Gardens'.

2. Takekoshi, *Prince Saionji*, p 93, states that Saionji was instrumental in the foundation of the Meiji Law School. However, the Meiji University website's own history does not mention him, instead concentrating on his fellow Francophiles Kishimoto Tatsuo, Miyagi Kōzō and Yashiro Misao, who had studied under Boissonade.

3. Takekoshi, *Prince Saionji*, p 95. Ōmura, *The Last Genrō*, pp 77–8, prefers the translation *Oriental Liberal Newspaper*. Production was suspended after issue #34 on 30 April 1881.

4. Iwai, *Saionji Kinmochi*, p 44.

5. It is worth noting here, as does Iwai, that the dates do not match. Declassified documents suggest that the news of the Emperor's command was delivered *after* Saionji's 'response'.

6. L Connors, *The Emperor's Adviser: Saionji Kinmochi and Pre-War Japanese Politics* (Croom Helm/Nissan Institute, London: 1987) p 7.

7. Richardson, *Judith Gautier*, pp 151, 286. Unlike earlier alleged collaborations with Gautier, the title page of *Poèmes de la Libellule* leaves nothing to doubt: 'Traduits du japonais d'après la version littérale de M. Saionzi [*sic*], Conseiller d'État de S.M. l'Empereur du Japon, par Judith Gautier.'

8. Takekoshi, *Prince Saionji*, p 118, has a confused and occasionally incoherent description of the incident. Saionji appeared to be acting on rumours of foreign movement in the Straits of Tsushima, which may have been caused by the establishment of a *British* naval base on Geomun-do, off Korea's south-west coast.

9. Ōmura, *The Last Genrō*, p 106. Ratification of the treaty was later postponed, after a bomb was thrown at the Japanese Foreign Minister in protest at the clause permitting foreigners to become Japanese citizens.

10. Takekoshi, *Prince Saionji*, p 122.

6: Japanism

1. Keene, *Emperor of Japan*, pp 446–54.

2. L Seaman, *From Tokio Through Manchuria with the Japanese* (D Appleton and Company, New York: 1905) p 65.

3. Takekoshi, *Prince Saionji*, p 124. 'Hare-foot-fern' is the translator's decision. Considering other slip-ups in the Takekoshi manuscript, it is possible that the original was not a hare-foot fern (*Davallia canariensis*), but the variant more common in Japan, *Davallia bullata*.

4. Ōmura, *The Last Genrō*, p 120.

5. Takekoshi, *Prince Saionji*, p 134.

6. W Beasley, *Japanese Imperialism 1894–1945* (Clarendon Press, Oxford: 1991) p 67.

7. Witte, quoted in Keene, *Emperor of Japan*, p 450.

8. Saionji, letter to Inoue Kaoru, quoted in Connors, *The Emperor's Adviser*, p 9.

9. R Hackett, *Yamagata Aritomo in the Rise of Modern Japan, 1838–1922* (Harvard University Press, Cambridge, MA: 1971) p 171.

7: The Yellow Peril

1. There is some disagreement over the precise events, as one might expect from a political assassination that was covered up, and a trial thrown out of court for 'lack of evidence'. I follow the account as reported in

Keene, *Emperor of Japan*, pp 516–17, but draw the reader's attention to the variants discussed in Keene's own endnotes. Dye was not the only witness – a Russian electrical engineer, Alexander Sabatin, wrote of the murders in his diary, which lay undiscovered until 1995.

2. Bonsal, *Suitors and Suppliants*, p 224.
3. Beasley, *Japanese Imperialism*, p 54.
4. Takekoshi, *Prince Saionji*, p 143.
5. Takekoshi, *Prince Saionji*, p 151. The text from the *Romance of the Three Kingdoms* is from chapter 56, section 43.
6. Takekoshi, *Prince Saionji*, p 153.
7. Connors, *The Emperor's Adviser*, p 11.
8. Connors, *The Emperor's Adviser*, p 15.
9. Takekoshi, *Prince Saionji*, p 233.
10. Takekoshi, *Prince Saionji*, p 219.
11. Connors, *The Emperor's Adviser*, p 21.
12. Takekoshi, *Prince Saionji*, p 223.
13. Takekoshi, *Prince Saionji*, p 224.
14. Takekoshi, *Prince Saionji*, p 236.
15. Connors, *The Emperor's Adviser*, p 27.
16. Beasley, *Japanese Imperialism*, pp 94–5.

8: The Taishō Crisis

1. Takekoshi, *Prince Saionji*, p 252; Connors, *The Emperor's Adviser*, p 33.
2. Takekoshi, *Prince Saionji*, p 257.
3. Beasley, *Japanese Imperialism*, pp 109–10.
4. Beasley, *Japanese Imperialism*, p 112.
5. E Selle, *Donald of China* (Harper and Brothers, New York: 1948) p 159. The envoy is named as 'Mr Funatsu' – no first name is supplied.

9: The Faults of the Past

1. Connors, *The Emperor's Adviser*, p 71.
2. Y Oka, *Prince Konoe Fumimaro: A Political Biography* (Madison Books, Lanham: 1992) p 15.
3. Konoe, 'Reject the Anglo-American-centred Peace', quoted in Oka, *Konoe Fumimaro*, pp 10–11.
4. Konoe, 'Reject the Anglo-American-centred Peace', quoted in Oka, *Konoe Fumimaro*, p 13.
5. Connors, *The Emperor's Adviser*, p 70.
6. R Fifield, *Woodrow Wilson and the Far East: The Diplomacy of the Shantung Question* (Thomas Y Crowell, New York: 1952) p 119.
7. Saionji, interview with *Le Petit Marseillais*, quoted in Connors, *The Emperor's Adviser*, p 69.
8. Connors, *The Emperor's Adviser*, p 69.
9. Clemenceau, *Grandeur and Misery of Victory*, p 140. One is tempted to suggest that Clemenceau's comment might have been mistranslated sarcasm, and that what he meant was: 'Makino… talks a lot, but says very little.' For his asides, see Fifield, *Woodrow Wilson and the Far East*, p 115, and MacMillan, *Paris 1919*, p 307.
10. MacMillan, *Paris 1919*, p 307.
11. Bonsal, *Suitors and Suppliants*, p 223.
12. Connors, *The Emperor's Adviser*, p 75.
13. Fifield, *Woodrow Wilson and the Far East*, p 206. Kim Kyusik or Gim Gyu-sik (1881–1950) was a Master's graduate from Princeton who would eventually rise to the position of Vice-President in Korea's provisional government. He was captured in the Korean War and died in unknown circumstances. I am indebted to Dr Koen De Ceuster of Leiden University for giving me a copy of his unpublished paper presented at the

British Academy on 7 December 2007, on 'The Korean Delegation at the 1907 Peace Conference in The Hague', which helped put much of the 1919 machinations in perspective.

14. Bonsal, *Suitors and Suppliants*, p 225.
15. Bonsal, *Suitors and Suppliants*, p 225.
16. Connors, *The Emperor's Adviser*, p 72. Both the King's reaction and Saionji's explanation were reported to Tokyo and leaked to Japanese newspapers. They were later denied by both governments, but supported by declassified documents including Fo.371.5350 F9/9/23.
17. Bonsal, *Suitors and Suppliants*, p 233.
18. Bonsal, *Suitors and Suppliants*, p 224.

10: The Anglo-American Peace

1. Ōmura, *The Last Genrō*, pp 351–2.
2. MacMillan, *Paris 1919*, p 315.
3. C Pearl, *Morrison of Peking* (Penguin Books, Melbourne: 1967) pp 374–5.
4. MacMillan, *Paris 1919*, p 315.
5. MacMillan, *Paris 1919*, p 103.
6. Fifield, *Woodrow Wilson and the Far East*, p 159.
7. David Hunter Miller, quoted in Fifield, *Woodrow Wilson and the Far East*, p 160.
8. MacMillan, *Paris 1919*, p 318.
9. MacMillan, *Paris 1919*, p 321.
10. Ōmura, *The Last Genrō*, p 354.

11: The Shandong Question

1. W King, *Woodrow Wilson, Wellington Koo and the China Question at the Paris Peace Conference* (A W Sythoff, Leyden: 1959) p 9.

2. Connors, *The Emperor's Adviser*, p 234.
3. Fifield, *Woodrow Wilson and the Far East*, p 256.
4. King, *Woodrow Wilson, Wellington Koo and the China Question at the Paris Peace Conference*, p 10.
5. P Chu, *V.K. Wellington Koo: A Case Study of China's Diplomat and Diplomacy of Nationalism 1912–1966* (Chinese University Press, Hong Kong: 1981) pp 55–6.
6. King, *Woodrow Wilson, Wellington Koo and the China Question at the Paris Peace Conference*, pp 21–2. See also Chu, *V.K. Wellington Koo*, p 76.
7. Chu, *V.K. Wellington Koo*, p 57.
8. R Lansing, *The Peace Negotiations: A Personal Narrative* (Constable, London: 1921) p 262.
9. Connors, *The Emperor's Adviser*, pp 69–70.

12: The Dark Valley

1. Oka, *Konoe Fumimaro*, pp 18–19.
2. Oka, *Konoe Fumimaro*, pp 23–4.
3. Harada, *Fragile Victory*, p 89.
4. Connors, *The Emperor's Adviser*, p 87.
5. Connors, *The Emperor's Adviser*, p 115.
6. Harada, *Fragile Victory*, p 85.
7. Connors, *The Emperor's Adviser*, p 125.
8. Connors, *The Emperor's Adviser*, p 128.
9. The precise identities of the bombers are still unknown. The Lytton Report commissioned by the League of Nations placed the blame squarely with the Japanese army, and this is the view widely held in modern times. At least one Japanese museum, at the controversial Yasukuni Shrine in Tokyo, still claims it was an act of Chinese aggression.
10. Connors, *The Emperor's Adviser*, p 131.

11. Connors, *The Emperor's Adviser*, p 132.

13: Last of the Genrō

1. Oka, *Konoe Fumimaro*, p 35.
2. Connors, *The Emperor's Adviser*, p 170.
3. Takekoshi, *Prince Saionji*, p 290.
4. Connors, *The Emperor's Adviser*, p 208.

Chronology

YEAR	AGE	LIFE
1849		7 Dec: Born as Tokudaiji Yoshimaru.
1851	2	Renamed Kinmochi, and adopted into the Saionji family as a 'real son'. Death of his stepfather Morosue: as his official heir, appointed a junior grade noble of the fifth rank.
1852	3	Death of Saionji's stepmother.
1853	4	Appointed Chamberlain. Arrival of Commodore Perry's 'Black Ships' in Japan.
1857	8	Inducted as the Minor General of the Right Imperial Guard.
1860	11	Ordered to attend the Imperial Palace, but is relieved of 'daily miscellaneous duties'. Bamboo hedge fire scare.
1861	12	Appointed Middle General of the Right Imperial Guard, and listed as one of the palace musicians.
1868	19	Meiji Restoration: after successful command of Imperial forces at Aizu, appointed Governor of Echigo.

YEAR	HISTORY	CULTURE
1849	British win Second Sikh War.	Charles Dickens, *David Copperfield*.
1851	Cuba declares its independence.	Herman Melville, *Moby Dick*.
	Victoria, Australia, proclaimed a separate colony.	John Ruskin, *The Stones of Venice*.
	Isaac Singer invents sewing machine.	
1852	French Second Empire declared.	Harriet Beecher Stowe, *Uncle Tom's Cabin*.
1853	Ottoman Empire declares war on Russia: Ottoman fleet destroyed at Sinope.	Charlotte Brontë, *Villette*. Elizabeth Gaskell, *Ruth* and *Cranford*.
1857	Outbreak of Indian Mutiny.	Baudelaire, *Les Fleurs du Mal*.
	Second Opium War.	Thomas Hughes, *Tom Brown's Schooldays*.
1860	Second Opium War: Anglo-French troops reach Beijing.	Wilkie Collins, *The Woman in White*.
	Abraham Lincoln elected US President.	George Eliot, *The Mill on the Floss*.
1861	Outbreak of American Civil War.	George Eliot, *Silas Marner*.
	Death of Prince Albert.	Mrs Beeton, *Book of Household Management*.
1868	British Abyssinian expedition.	Wilkie Collins, *The Moonstone*.
	Ulysses S Grant elected US President.	Wagner, opera 'Die Meistersinger von Nürnberg'.

YEAR	AGE	LIFE
1869	20	Resigns governorship; returns to Tokyo.
		Offers to marry a woman of the underclass.
		Establishment of the Ritsumei group (eventually Ritsumeikan)
1871	22	Commencement of the Iwakura Mission.
		Goes to France, where he stays for nine years: arrives in Paris a few days before the Paris Commune.
		Leaves after the suppression of the Commune for Geneva. Studies French in Nice and Marseilles, before returning to Paris.
1873	24	Declines his government allowance and becomes a private student.
		Begins an association with a woman of 'unknown character'.
		Works in an unofficial capacity at the Japanese Legation in Paris.
1877	28	The Japanese Legation in Paris secretly outbids Saigō Takamori at local arms dealers.
		Collaborates with Judith Gautier on *La Marchande de Sourires*.
1880	31	Returns to Japan.
		Lectures at the newly established Meiji Law School (later Meiji University)
1881	32	Publication of the *Eastern Liberal News* (*Tōyō Jiyū Shinbun*): ordered to resign from his position at the newspaper.
1882	33	Asked by Itō Hirobumi to accompany him on his mission to Europe.

YEAR	HISTORY	CULTURE
1883	The French gain control of Tunis. British decide to evacuate the Sudan. The Orient Express (Paris-Constantinople) makes its first run.	Death of Wagner. Nietzsche, *Thus Spake Zarathustra*.
1884	General Gordon arrives in Khartoum. Germans occupy South-West Africa.	Mark Twain, *Huckleberry Finn*. Seurat, painting 'Une Baignade à Asnières'.
1885	General Gordon killed in fall of Khartoum to the Mahdi. Germany annexes Tanganyika and Zanzibar.	Judith Gautier publishes *Poèmes de la Libellule*, based on translations by Saionji. Gilbert and Sullivan, operetta 'The Mikado'.
1886	First Indian National Congress meets. Canadian-Pacific Railway completed.	R L Stevenson, *Dr Jekyll and Mr Hyde*. Marx's *Das Kapital* published in English.
1887	First Colonial Conference in London. Queen Victoria's Golden Jubilee. Failed coup by General Boulanger in Paris.	Pierre Loti, *Madame Chrysanthème*. Van Gogh, painting 'Moulin de la Galette'.
1891	Nicholas Alexandrovitch, the future Tsar Nicholas II, is attacked in Ōtsu, Japan. Triple Alliance (Austria-Hungary, Germany, Italy) renewed for 12 years. Franco-Russian entente.	Thomas Hardy, *Tess of the D'Urbervilles*. Mahler, Symphony No 1.

YEAR	AGE	LIFE
1893	44	Appointed Vice President of the House of Peers.
1894	45	20 Aug: becomes special envoy to the Korean king. 3 Sep: becomes Minister of Education.
1896	47	Proposes to publish *Japan in the World*, magazine. Also created Foreign Minister in addition to Minister of Education. Resignation of Itō's cabinet.
1897	48	Travels to France. Contracts acute appendicitis.
1898	49	Jan-Jun: Education Minister in third Itō cabinet.
1900	51	Founder-member of Ito's Rikken Seiyūkai party. Has no post in fourth Itō cabinet but attends meetings in his new role as President of the Privy Council. Serves as Acting Prime Minister during Itō's illness.
1901	52	Appointed Acting Prime Minister for four weeks following the resignation of the Itō cabinet.

YEAR	HISTORY	CULTURE
1893	France acquires protectorate over Laos.	Oscar Wilde, *A Woman of No Importance*.
	Benz constructs his four-wheel car.	Puccini, opera 'Manon Lescaut'.
1894	Sino-Japanese War begins: Japanese defeat Chinese at Port Arthur.	G & W Grossmith, *The Diary of a Nobody*.
	Dreyfus Case begins in France.	Anthony Hope, *The Prisoner of Zenda*.
1896	Failure of Jameson Raid: Kaiser Wilhelm II sends 'Kruger Telegram'.	Chekhov, *The Seagull*.
	Kitchener begins reconquest of the Sudan.	Richard Strauss, symphonic poem 'Also Sprach Zarathustra'.
	Russia and China sign Manchurian Convention.	Puccini, opera 'La Bohème'.
		Nobel Prizes established.
1897	Queen Victoria's Diamond Jubilee.	H G Wells, *The Invisible Man*.
	Russia occupies Port Arthur.	Edmond Rostand, *Cyrano de Bergerac*.
1898	Spanish-American War.	Thomas Hardy, *Wessex Poems*.
	Death of Bismarck.	Henry James, *The Turn of the Screw*.
1900	Second Boer War: relief of Mafeking and capture of Johannesburg and Pretoria.	Freud, *The Interpretation of Dreams*.
	Assassination of King Umberto I of Italy.	Puccini, *Tosca*.
	Boxer Rising in China.	Joseph Conrad, *Lord Jim*.
		Sargent, *The Sitwell Family*.
1901	Death of Queen Victoria: US President McKinley is assassinated: Theodore Roosevelt sworn in as President.	First five Nobel Prizes awarded.
		Rudyard Kipling, *Kim*.

YEAR	AGE	LIFE
1903	54	The former Kyoto Hōsei School is renamed Ritsumeikan with his permission. Becomes the leader of the Seiyūkai.
1904	55	Birth of second daughter, Sonoko, to another geisha mistress. Outbreak of Russo-Japanese War.
1905	56	End of Russo-Japanese War Treaty of Portsmouth
1906	57	Marriage of daughter Shinko to Mōri Hachirō. Hachirō takes the Saionji surname. Birth of grandson Kinkazu. Serves first proper term as Prime Minister of Japan (until 1908).
1910	61	Birth of Saionji's grandson Fujio
1911	62	Serves another term as Prime Minister of Japan (until 1912) Republican Revolution in China.
1913	64	Appointed *genrō* after resignation as Prime Minister. Ritsumeikan becomes Ritsumeikan University.

YEAR	HISTORY	CULTURE
1903	King Edward VII visits Paris – beginning of Entente Cordiale. Wright Brothers' first flight.	Henry James, *The Ambassadors*. Film: *The Great Train Robbery*.
1904	Roosevelt wins US Presidential election.	J M Barrie, *Peter Pan*. Premiere of Puccini's 'Madame Butterfly' in Milan.
1905	'Bloody Sunday' – Russian demonstration broken-up by police. Tsar Nicholas II issues the 'October Manifesto'.	E M Forster, *Where Angels Fear to Tread*.
1906	Edward VII of England and Kaiser Wilhelm II of Germany meet. Major earthquake in San Francisco USA kills over 1,000.	John Galsworthy, *A Man of Property*. Invention of first jukebox.
1910	King Edward VII dies; succeeded by George V.	E M Forster, *Howard's End*. H G Wells, *The History of Mr. Polly*.
1911	Arrival of German gunboat *Panther* in Agadir triggers international crisis. Republican revolution in China.	D H Lawrence, *The White Peacock*. Strauss, opera 'Der Rosenkavalier'.
1913	Second Balkan war breaks out. US Federal Reserve System is established.	Thomas Mann, *Death in Venice*. Grand Central Station in New York is completed.

YEAR	AGE	LIFE
1919	70	Heads Japanese delegation at the Paris Peace Conference: retains Pacific Islands taken from Germany, and Shandong, but fails to get racial equality clause into League of Nations charter.
1920	71	Created a Prince in recognition of a lifetime's service.
1931	82	Manchurian Incident: fails to stop invasion of Manchuria winning support at home.
1932	83	Opposes Japanese walkout from League of Nations over League's refusal to recognise puppet state of Manchukuo, but to no avail
1936	87	February 26 Incident: refuses to flee during uprising. Proposes Konoe Fumimaro as Prime Minister.
1940	90	24 Nov: Dies.

YEAR	HISTORY	CULTURE
1919	Communist Revolt in Berlin. Benito Mussolini founds fascist movement in Italy. US Senate votes against ratification of Versailles Treaty, leaving the USA outside the League of Nations.	Thomas Hardy, *Collected Poems*. Herman Hesse, *Demian*. George Bernard Shaw, *Heartbreak House*. Film: *The Cabinet of Dr Caligari*.
1920	League of Nations comes into existence: headquarters moved to Geneva. Bolsheviks win Russian Civil War.	F Scott Fitzgerald, *This Side of Paradise*. Franz Kafka, *The Country Doctor*.
1931	Bankruptcy of Credit-Anstalt in Austria begins financial collapse of Central Europe. National Government formed in Great Britain.	Robert Frost, *Collected Poems*. Films: *Dracula. Little Caesar*.
1932	F D Roosevelt wins US Presidential election in Democrat landslide. Kurt von Schleicher forms ministry in Germany attempting to conciliate Centre and Left.	Aldous Huxley, *Brave New World*. Films: *Grand Hotel. Tarzan the Ape Man*.
1936	German troops reoccupy Rhineland. Abdication Crisis. Outbreak of Spanish Civil War.	J M Keynes, *General Theory of Employment, Interest and Money*. Berlin Olympics. Films: *Modern Times. Camille. The Petrified Forest. Things to Come*
1940	Second World War. The Battle of Britain. Roosevelt is elected for an unprecedented third term.	Eugene O'Neill, *Long Days Journey into Night*. Films: *The Great Dictator. Pinocchio*.

Further Reading

Saionji was one of the first Meiji-era figures to receive a full-length English-language biography, lionised in a 1933 study published by Ritsumeikan, the university he helped to found. And yet even his biographer Takekoshi Yosaburō reports his subject's unwillingness to discuss personal information. 'I several times attempted to write a sketch of the Prince and asked him questions, but he would not talk about himself and even when he was obliged to speak about his part in certain affairs he quickly turned his talk to the present and the future.' Despite this reticence from its subject, Takekoshi's account is respectful but also informative and rewarding, although the English translation can be misleadingly imprecise. Ōmura Bunji's *The Last Genrō*, published five years later, is just as problematic, since it adopts a style, infuriatingly common in Japanese historical writing, that invents scenes and dialogue that the author cannot possibly have witnessed, turning Saionji's life into a historical novel. Entirely devoid of footnotes, it offers many interesting anecdotes and often implies inside knowledge, but offers little that a historian can fully trust. English materials improve once Saionji was an elder statesman in the 20th century – the best and most concise examination of Saionji's later career is Lesley Connors' *The Emperor's Adviser*.

Japanese readers have a wider choice of material, most recently with Iwai Tadakuma's robust 2003 biography. Iwai's direct, modern Japanese is a welcome relief from the circumlocutions of earlier books (it is even clearer than some English texts!), but is sadly a little too concise for in-depth study of particular areas of his life. Its coverage of the Paris Peace Conference, for example, is limited to a mere handful of pages. An embarrassment of riches awaits in the form of the memoirs of Count Harada Kumao, whose nine-volume account of Saionji's last decade presents a priceless record of the old diplomat's indirect method of information-gathering and subtle diplomacy. Known as the *Saionji-Harada Memoirs*, the entire colossus was translated into English as part of the military tribunal that followed the end of the Second World War, eventually forming a piece of court evidence totalling an impressive 3,286 pages, and still available on microfilm at specialist research institutions. Its first volume, largely concerned with the London Treaty of 1930, was made more widely available under the title *Fragile Victory*. Books by Oka Yoshitaka and Yagami Kazuo study the brash Prince Konoe, whose *angst* and attitude at Versailles prefigured Japan's own rush into militarism – the latter homing in on that crucial period a generation after Versailles, when the stumbling peace finally failed and Japan went to war.

The landmark work, of course, on Versailles is Margaret MacMillan's *Peacemakers*, published in the USA as *Paris 1919*, presumably to avoid confusion for gun enthusiasts. When it comes to the 'little nations' among which Japan was included, MacMillan leans heavily on Stephen Bonsal's *Suitors and Suppliants*, which includes several illuminating stories of

Saionji's actions. Whereas Saionji was a diligent proponent of peace, he was forced to represent a militarist government whose acts in the 1914–18 war had little to do with him, often leading his rival Paris Peace Conference delegates to brush him off as just another warmonger. It is worth noting that much of Saionji's Paris Conference activities were concerned with Japan's interests in China, and consequently a different perspective on Japanese diplomacy can be obtained through reading Chinese accounts of the same events. For these, the reader is directed to the biography of the Chinese delegate *Wellington Koo*, also in the Makers of the Modern World series.

For a general view of the environment that created Saionji and his colleagues, there is no better book than Donald Keene's authoritative biography of Meiji: *Emperor of Japan*. A very different perspective on the same era can be found in Lesley Downer's *Madame Sadayakko: The Geisha Who Seduced the West*, the biography of another star of the age of *japonisme*, who was also Itō Hirobumi's teenage mistress in the 1880s.

Beasley, W, *Japanese Imperialism 1894–1945* (Clarendon Press, Oxford: 1991).

Bonsal, S, *Unfinished Business* (Michael Joseph, London: 1944).

——, *Suitors and Suppliants* (Prentice-Hall, New York: 1946).

Chu, P, V.K. *Wellington Koo: A Case Study of China's Diplomat and Diplomacy of Nationalism 1912–1966* (Chinese University Press, Hong Kong: 1981).

Clemenceau, G, *Grandeur and Misery of Victory* (George Harrap, London: 1930).

Clements, J, *Makers of the Modern World – Wellington Koo, China* (Haus Publishing, London: 2008).

Connors, L, *The Emperor's Adviser: Saionji Kinmochi and Pre-War Japanese Politics* (Croom Helm/Nissan Institute, London: 1987).

Daniels, R, *The Politics of Prejudice: the Anti-Japanese Movement in California and the Struggle for Japanese Exclusion* (University of California Press, Berkeley: 1977).

Downer, L, *Madame Sadayakko: The Geisha Who Seduced the West* (Review, London: 2003).

Feifer, G, *Breaking Open Japan: Commodore Perry, Lord Abe and American Imperialism in 1853* (Harper Collins, New York: 2006).

Fifield, R, *Woodrow Wilson and the Far East: The Diplomacy of the Shantung Question* (Thomas Y Crowell, New York: 1952).

Gautier, J, *La Soeur du Soleil / L'Usurpateur* (L'Harmattan, Paris: 2006 [facsimile of 1887 edition]).

Hackett, R, *Yamagata Aritomo in the Rise of Modern Japan, 1838–1922* (Harvard University Press, Cambridge, MA: 1971).

Harada, K, *Saionji-ko to Seikyoku [Prince Saionji and the Political Situation]*, in 9 volumes (Iwanami Shoten, Tokyo: 1950–6).

——, *Fragile Victory: Prince Saionji and the 1930 London Treaty Issue from the Memoirs of Baron Harada Kumao* (Wayne State University Press, Detroit: 1968).

Iwai, T, *Saionji Kinmochi: Saigo no Genrō* (Iwanami Shoten, Tokyo: 2003).

Keene, D, *Emperor of Japan: Meiji and His World, 1852–1912* (Columbia University Press, New York: 2002).

King, W, *Woodrow Wilson, Wellington Koo and the China Question at the Paris Peace Conference* (A W Sythoff, Leyden: 1959).

Lansing, R, *The Peace Negotiations: A Personal Narrative* (Constable, London: 1921).

MacMillan, M, *Paris 1919* (John Murray, London: 2001).

Mutsu, M, *Kenkenroku: A Diplomatic Record of the Sino-Japanese War, 1894–1895* (Princeton University Press, Princeton: 1982).

Najita, T, *Japan: The Intellectual Foundations of Modern Japanese Politics* (University of Chicago Press, Chicago: 1974).

Nakae, C, *A Discourse by Three Drunkards on Government*, 1887 [trans. Nobuko Tsukui] (Weatherhill, New York: 1984).

Nish, I, *The Origins of the Russo-Japanese War* (Longman, London: 1985).

Oka, Y, *Prince Konoe Fumimaro: A Political Biography* (Madison Books, Lanham: 1992).

Ōmura, B, *The Last Genrō – Prince Saionji: The Man Who Westernized Japan* (J B Lippincott Company, Philadelphia: 1938).

Pearl, C, *Morrison of Peking* (Penguin Books, Melbourne: 1967).

Richardson, J, *Judith Gautier: A Biography* (Quartet Books, London: 1986).

Seaman, L, *From Tokio Through Manchuria with the Japanese* (D Appleton and Company, New York: 1905).

Selle, E, *Donald of China* (Harper and Brothers, New York: 1948).

Takekoshi, Y, *Prince Saionji* (Ritsumeikan University, Kyoto: 1933).

Yagami, Kazuo, *Konoe Fumimaro and the Failure of Peace in Japan, 1937–1941: A Critical Appraisal of the Three-time Prime Minister* (McFarland, Jefferson: 2006).

Picture Sources

The author and publishers wish to express their thanks to the following sources of illustrative material and/or permission to reproduce it. They will make proper acknowledgements in future editions in the event that any omissions have occurred.

Getty Images: p. 146. Topham Picturepoint pp. 10, 108.

Endpapers

The Signing of Peace in the Hall of Mirrors, Versailles, 28th June 1919 by Sir William Orpen (Bridgeman Art Library)
Front row: Dr Johannes Bell (Germany) signing with Herr Hermann Müller leaning over him
Middle row (seated, left to right): General Tasker H Bliss, Col E M House, Mr Henry White, Mr Robert Lansing, President Woodrow Wilson (United States); M Georges Clemenceau (France); Mr David Lloyd George, Mr Andrew Bonar Law, Mr Arthur J Balfour, Viscount Milner, Mr G N Barnes (Great Britain); Prince Saionji (Japan)
Back row (left to right): M Eleftherios Venizelos (Greece); Dr Afonso Costa (Portugal); Lord Riddell (British Press);

Sir George E Foster (Canada); M Nikola Pašić (Serbia);
M Stephen Pichon (France); Col Sir Maurice Hankey,
Mr Edwin S Montagu (Great Britain); the Maharajah of
Bikaner (India); Signor Vittorio Emanuele Orlando (Italy);
M Paul Hymans (Belgium); General Louis Botha (South
Africa); Mr W M Hughes (Australia)

Jacket Images

(Front): akg Images.
(Back): *Peace Conference at the Quai d'Orsay* by Sir
William Orpen (akg Images).
Left to right (seated): Signor Orlando (Italy); Mr Robert
Lansing, President Woodrow Wilson (United States); M
Georges Clemenceau (France); Mr David Lloyd George, Mr
Andrew Bonar Law, Mr Arthur J Balfour (Great Britain);
Left to right (standing): M Paul Hymans (Belgium); Mr
Eleftherios Venizelos (Greece); The Emir Feisal (The
Hashemite Kingdom); Mr W F Massey (New Zealand);
General Jan Smuts (South Africa); Col E M House (United
States); General Louis Botha (South Africa); Prince Saionji
(Japan); Mr W M Hughes (Australia); Sir Robert Borden
(Canada); Mr G N Barnes (Great Britain); M Ignacy
Paderewski (Poland)

Index

A

Acollas, Émile 47–8, 55, 86,
163
Anglo-Satsuma War
24–5
Australia 130, 131, 131

B

Balfour, Arthur 100, 132
Bismarck, Otto von 66–7
Bismarck Archipelago, the
130
Bonsal, Stephen 1–2, 83–4,
122, 124–5, 142
Boxer Rebellion, the 87

C

Caroline Islands 130
Cecil, Robert 130, 133
Chiang Kai-shek 152,
158

Chichibu, Prince 164
China 64–5, 72–3, 74–7, 87,
97–8, 100–1, 152–3
Shandong Peninsula
137–44
Twenty-One Demands,
the 102–4
Chinda Sutemi 111, 112–13,
122, 132, 140
Clemenceau, Georges 48,
49, 56, 120, 129, 134,
140, 142
Convention of Tianjin, the
72, 73

D

Daewon-gun, the 73–4,
81–2
Ding Ruchang 65
Duan Qirui 105
Dye, William M 83

E

*Eastern Liberal News see
    Tōyō Jiyū Shinbun*

F

February 26 Incident 163–4
First World War, the 100–2,
    106
Fourteen Points, the
    117–19, 123
France 28, 29, 40–1, 44–52
Franco-Prussian War, the
    44–5
Fushimi Hiroyasu, Fleet
    Admiral Prince 154,
    164

G

Gautier, Judith 50–2
George V, King 125, 149
Germany 62–3, 101–2, 137
Gojong, King 73, 81, 84
Grant, President Ulysses S
    43
Great Britain 21, 24–5, 28,
    29, 88–9

H

Hanoteaux, Gabriel 85
Hara Kei 111–12
Harada Kumao 167
Harris, Townsend 21

Hirohito, Emperor 150–2,
    167
    European tour 151
    February 26 Incident
        163–4
House, Colonel Edward 2,
    120, 132
Hughes, Billy 130, 131, 133

I

Ii Naosuke 24
Inukai Tsuyoshi 161
Ishii Kikujurō 104, 131
Itō Hirobumi 61, 64, 70–1,
    78, 86, 87
Iwakura Tomomi 24, 32,
    47

J

Japan
    Anglo-Japanese
        Alliance 88
    Anglo-Satsuma War
        24–5
    coup attempts 155, 161,
        163–4
    Delegation to Peace
        Conference 111–17,
        117, 120
    Diet created 60–1
    first opening to the
        West 18–21

First Sino-Japanese War
73, 74–5, 85
First World War 100–2,
104
former German
possessions 128–31
'Hidden Christians',
the 32
immigration to USA
93–4
Lancing-Ishii
Agreement, the
104–5
League of Nations,
attitude to 135–6,
143, 158–9
Manchuria 89, 95–6, 98,
152–3, 155–8
Meiji Restoration, the
31–9
militarism 99–100,
158–9
racial equality 116, 128,
131–6, 141–
Russo-Japanese War,
the 89–91, 106
Second Sino-Japanese
War 166
Second World War, the
166–7
Siberian Intervention,
the 106

Treaty of Amity and
Commerce (US)
21
Treaty of Anglo-
Japanese Friendship
21
Treaty of Portsmouth
89–91, 106
Triple Intervention, the
77–9, 84
Twenty-One Demands,
the 102–4
Japonisme 50–2
Jiaozhou 138

K
Kan'in, house of 14–15
Katsura Tarō 7, 86, 88, 91,
92, 96, 97, 99, 106
Kim Kyusik 124
Kim Ok-gyun 72
Kōmei, Emperor 25–6, 28
Kōmyōji Saburō 49–50, 51
Konoe Fumimaro 113–17,
127, 140, 149–50, 159,
161–2, 165–6
Koo, Wellington 137–9
and Woodrow Wilson
138, 141
Korea 72–4, 81–5, 150
and the Peace
Conference 122–5

L

Lancing, Robert 104
Lancing-Ishii Agreement,
    the 104–5
League of Nations, the 115,
    116, 124, 131–6, 143,
    151, 154, 158
Li Hongzhang 64, 75–7
Liaodong Peninsula, the 75,
    78, 89
Lloyd George, David 120,
    131, 134, 141
London Naval Conference
    154

M

Makino Nobuaki 100, 103,
    112, 122, 132–4, 135,
    138, 140, 141, 161
Manchukuo see Manchuria
Manchuria 89, 95–6, 98,
    152–3, 155–8
Manchurian Incident 156–7
Marianas Islands 130
Marshall Islands 130
Matsui Keishiro 113, 140
Meiji Emperor, the 23, 27,
    77, 98
Meiji Restoration, the 31–9,
    69
Min, Queen 73, 82–3, 122,
    153

Miura Gorō 81–3
Morrison, George 128–9
Mutsu Munemitsu 74–5,
    78, 80
Mutsuhito, Prince see the
    Meiji Emperor

N

Nakae Chōmin 48–9, 55, 58
Nakashima Sōin 16
Nicholas II, Tsar 69–70,
    77–8
Nicholas Alexandrovich,
    Prince see Tsar Nicholas
    II

O

Ōkuma Shigenobu 61
Orlando, Vittorio 120

P

Pak, General 124
Paris Commune, the 45–6
Parkes, Sir Harry 32
Perry, Commodore
    Matthew Calbraith
    18–19, 20
Pescadores Islands 75
Putiatin, Vice-Admiral
    Evfemy Vasilyevich
    19–21
Puyi (the 'Last Emperor') 97

Q

Qingdao 102

R

racial equality 116, 131–6,
141–2
Richardson, Charles
Lennox 24
Roosevelt, President
Theodore 89–90, 94
Russia 19–21, 77–8, 84,
89–91, 105, 125–6
Russo-Japanese War, the
89–91, 106
Treaty of Portsmouth,
the 89–91, 106

S

Saigō Takamori 52
Saionji Kinmochi
Acting Prime Minister
87–8
adoption 15–16
ambassador to
Germany 65–7
and Clemenceau 49, 56,
140–1
birth 13
courtier 16, 23–4
death 166
February 26 Incident
163

Foreign Minister 76–7,
79, 84
founds Ritsumeikan 40
founds *Tōyō Jiyū
Shinbun* 56–60
francophilia 3, 5–6,
40–1, 122
genrō 99–100
George V, meeting with
149
head of Peace
Conference
delegation 111–12,
127
Hirohito's regency
150–1
Itō mission, the 62–3
Korean mission 73–
law lecturer 55–6
London Naval
Conference 154–5
Meiji Restoration 34–9
Minister of Education
74, 79, 80
Minister to Austria-
Hungary 64
Movement to Protect
Constitutional
Government 99
Prime Minister 91–6,
98–9
resignation as *genrō*

Russian claims in
   Mediterranean
   125–6
Satsuma Rebellion 52
studies in Paris 44–53
trial of the Kaiser 125,
   149
visits London 43
visits USA 42–3
Western habits 41
Saitō Makoto, Admiral 162
Sakura-kai (Cherry
   Blossom Society) 155
Satsuma Rebellion 52
Shandong Peninsula 101–2,
   105, 137–44
Second World War, the
   166–7
Siberian Intervention, the
   106
Sino-Japanese War
   First 73, 74–5, 85
   Second 166
Smuts, Jan 130

T
Taishō Emperor, the 98, 150
Taiwan 75
Takatsukasa Masamichi 32
Tianjin 75
Tōgō Heihachirō, Admiral
   151

Tokugawa Nariaki 24
Tōyō Jiyū Shinbun (*Eastern
   Liberal News*) 56–60
Triple Intervention, the
   77–9, 84
Twenty-One Demands, the
   102–4, 138

U
Ukagi, General 155
United States, the 18–19, 29,
   43, 89–90
   and Japanese
      immigration 93–5,
      129–30
   Lancing-Ishii
      Agreement, the
      104–5

V
Venizelos, Eleftherios 133

W
Watanabe Chiaki 87
Weihaiwei 75
Wilhelm II, Kaiser 66–7,
   125
Wilson, Woodrow 105–6,
   120, 140
   Japan and Korea 124
   racial equality clause
      134–6, 141–2

Pacific islands 129–30
Shandong question
141–3
Wellington Koo 138,
141
Witte, Count Sergei 78

Y
Yamagata Aritomo 86, 113

Yamaguchi Motoomi,
Lieutenant-General 87
Yuan Shikai 98, 101, 103

Z
Zhang Zuolin 152–3